MAKING
MARKETING
WORK

MAKING MARKETING WORK

A Step by Step Guide for New Businesses

**Gerard Earls and
Patrick Forsyth**

Published in Association with
The Institute of Chartered Accountants
in England and Wales

KOGAN
PAGE

First published in Great Britain in 1989 by Kogan Page Limited, 120 Pentonville
Road, London N1 9JN.

British Library Cataloguing in Publication Data

Earls, Gerard
   Making marketing work.—(Business enterprise guides).
   1. Marketing
   I. Title II. Forsyth, Patrick III. Institute of Chartered Accountants in
   England and Wales IV. Series
   658.8   HF5415

   ISBN 1–85091–533–4
   ISBN 1–85091–530–X Pbk

Printed and bound in Great Britain by
Biddles Limited, Guildford

Acknowledgements

'Gerry did most of the work'
'Patrick made me'

No one writing about marketing can know all the facts and write unaided. Marketing is a dynamic process. Marketing approaches and techniques change constantly, not least in response to market changes, competitive factors and what ever-demanding customers think at any particular moment.

Getting marketing right and regarding it as static thereafter is simply not one of the options.

So, in writing this book we have, necessarily, drawn on a variety of experiences and owe thanks to many colleagues and attendees on training courses, long and short, which we have conducted. Cumulatively, all have contributed and made this book possible. In particular, it has been made possible by many in small businesses, some whose situations are quoted, who have provided insights into the problems of starting and running such a business, and which have enriched our thinking.

From all these we have acquired a fascination and enthusiasm for marketing, which we have enjoyed enormously, and we hope some of this will be conveyed to you through this book.

Gerard Earls
Patrick Forsyth
Marketing Improvements Group,
Ulster House, 17 Ulster Terrace,
Outer Circle, Regent's Park,
London NW1 4PJ

Contents

Appendices

Preface

'. . . changed, changed utterly . . .'

W B Yeats
Easter 1916

Something remarkable is happening in Britain. And it represents a major opportunity for some.

Despite the problems of Britain's economic past, as the realities of the post-1974 recession are accepted, some real ways forward are becoming clear. It has become painfully clear that large organisations and nationalised industries can no longer provide cradle-to-the-grave job security, but are themselves having to adjust to changed demand. And that we can no longer rely on finding foreign firms anxious to set up in Britain and thus provide instant solutions to unemployment.

At the same time, examples abound of individuals and firms who do succeed in the harsher reality of today. When traditional industry retreats from whole areas, self-help is the only alternative to prolonged unemployment. Even professions that seemed insulated from market forces, such as accountancy, stockbroking and the law, are now, with great difficulty and some distaste, learning the arts of finding and keeping clients and competing with others in the same profession.

Important among the successes are small businesses, often set up in areas which, it might have been assumed, were open only to the big organisations. Yet they have by no means all been swamped; many have flourished; and many more are poised to do the same.

For these new entrepreneurs, setting up on their own can be the most rewarding step they ever take, although of course there are difficulties. Marketing is one of the elements of such a business that must be got right. This book is meant to help those who already belong to this number, or wish to join them, to do just that.

The new entrepreneur

Entrepreneurs new to business generally have a set of skills or technical expertise they wish to exploit. Strangely enough, it is the authors' experience that marketing skills are seldom high on this list. Those who have spent most of their lives in a large firm or a public utility and are now setting up by themselves become aware of this lack of expertise at an early stage. In their previous job, they may have enjoyed a steady demand for their services and have not had to spend any of their day ensuring that the orders or the cash continued to flow in, in a steady stream. They were concerned with costs and not with profits. As a result:

- they often have great difficulty in balancing supply and demand and are hurt to find that when they are overloaded customers will not wait but will place their business elsewhere;
- they may understand the costs of producing the product or service they are offering but often have little idea of how to set a price;
- since they underestimate the effort required to market their product or service, they neither allow time for it nor budget adequately for it in their costs;
- whereas the quality of product or standard of service was laid down for them in their previous job, they may now have to adjust quality upward to meet higher customer expectations or downward to meet price competition, and this is not an easy skill to master;
- it comes as a shock to realise that it is not sufficient simply to carry out the work involved but that a service mentality is necessary in each aspect of the firm. In a competitive market, the customer expects the firm to be concerned that what it is producing meets the customer's needs.

Much marketing literature is not very helpful in this situation. The majority has been written for the American market and tries to meet the demand for student textbooks – business degrees are far more common in the US. It assumes, therefore:

- that the firm is likely to be engaged in manufacture;
- that the reader has access to substantial human or financial

resources;
- that the reader is fascinated by theory, since he or she is a student of business, interested in passing examinations.

The authors believe that the new entrepreneur faces a different situation. One in which:

- a substantial proportion of new entrepreneurs will operate in service trades such as restaurants, retailing, construction, bookkeeping, photography. Marketing in such firms is appreciably different from marketing in what are referred to as fast-moving consumer goods (or FMCG), such as washing powders. In specific terms, the promotion, pricing and differentiation of a small business from its rivals needs a somewhat different approach;
- a small firm cannot rely on having substantial finances to be able to afford sophisticated marketing techniques. As in all other aspects of the business, every activity needs to be cost-effective and concentrate upon essentials. For example:

  - Market research should concentrate on providing essential information by using data that is cheap to obtain and relevant to the problem in hand.
  - Sales promotion needs to be appropriate, well thought out and well co-ordinated.
  - Those firms who get their business primarily through tenders or competitive presentations need to know how to structure their bid and present it with conviction.
  - Most entrepreneurs are very busy people. When they do have the luxury of snatching a moment to read a book, they need a format that is clear so that they can pick up the thread after any interruption. The concepts need to be stripped of unnecessary complications and deal with problems central to small business. Real-life examples taken from businesses of a comparable size are more helpful than abstractions.

Layout of this book

The structure of the book springs from what the authors believe the nature of marketing to be, in all senses of the word:

- Marketing is a management skill of fundamental importance to the survival of the firm.

- Marketing is a set-up of techniques and activities that interlock into a sequence to form a cohesive series of steps.
- Marketing decisions can be divided, on the one hand, into decisions that have designated '*internal considerations*'. These are the central decisions that keep the firm alive.
- On the other hand, marketing embraces a set of decisions designated the '*external considerations*'. These enable the entrepreneur to communicate with and influence the market using the channels and media available.

The interrelationship of these components is illustrated in Figure 1. The sequence of the chapters follows this cycle and is arranged in four parts.

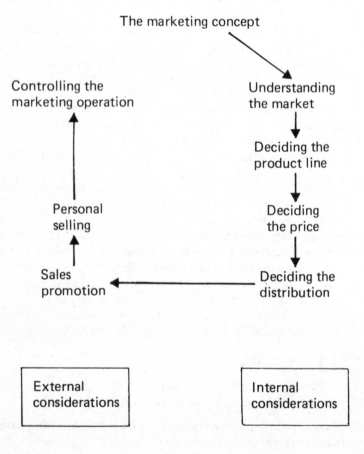

Figure 1. *The components of marketing*

Part 1. Introduction to Marketing
This section shows how the marketing concepts help you to define your business, and identify the major threats and opportunities. It also helps you to understand how the various elements of marketing fit together.

Part 2. The Internal Considerations
This section is to help you gather information and use it to take the critical decisions upon which the future of your business may well depend. The sequence is:

Understanding the Market Dynamics. This chapter shows you how to break down your market into segments so that you can concentrate your efforts most effectively. It also illustrates the processes your customers go through in choosing a product or service as a consumer or as a commercial or industrial buyer.

Researching the Market. This shows you how to carry out market research effectively, getting the best return for the money you spend on this activity.

The Marketing Plan. This helps you to develop a forecast which you need for your company plan. It also introduces the major marketing variables, which are treated in further depth in the chapters that follow.

The Product Plan. Having decided at which part of the market you will direct your efforts, you can now decide upon a range of services or products to meet customer needs.

The Pricing Decision. The procedure described in this chapter will help you to arrive at the most appropriate pricing strategy to realise the full profit-earning capability of your business.

Distribution. Unless the product or service is readily available to your target customers, they will choose a substitute and your product will fail. This chapter addresses the question of whether to market direct or use intermediaries. If you are to use intermediaries, you will need to persuade them to stock your product and give you continuing support. The chapter shows how this is done.

Part 3. The External Considerations
This section helps you to communicate with the influence your market using the channels and media available. The sequence is:

The Promotional Mix. The mysteries of public relations, advertising, direct mail, sales promotion, merchandising, sales literature and personal selling are dealt with as an integrated process which moves the customer towards the buying decision. The chapter concentrates on media that are not dependent upon large investments of cash.

Personal Selling. For many small businesses, this is the principal means of securing business. This chapter uses a step-by-step approach to help you master the essential skills.

Part 4. Synthesis and Conclusion
The book begins by setting standards and objectives. Then it looks at the internal considerations and, finally, the external considerations, including how to influence the market. The final chapter, *Controlling the Market Operation*, helps you to install uncomplicated processes to track how successful your marketing activities have been. Where you have not achieved the results you wanted, the inadequacies will show up and help to indicate what steps you should take to put things right.

Before you start reading this book

Do bear in mind that marketing does not simply consist of a set of rules that will guarantee success. It is a highly creative activity and calls for an inquisitive mind to arrive at opportunities that others have not spotted. It also requires the courage to implement new and fresh ways of exploiting them.

The book has been structured, however, to help you use it to develop your business. Examples derived from the businesses of new entrepreneurs have been used throughout. These are real firms and real people with whom the authors have worked. The names and details are disguised, however, so that the firms should not be recognisable to any but the people who own them. Although no two business ideas are the same, it is hoped that some resemble your situation sufficiently closely to start you on a chain of ideas and solutions of your own. At the end of each chapter, you are invited to reflect on how the principles discussed in the text could apply to your business. You may find it useful to consider the questionnaire immediately and then come back in a few months' time to measure what progress you have made in implementing some of these ideas. In this way, good ideas can be translated into financial results.

Part 1
Introduction to Marketing

1
The Marketing Challenge

What does marketing mean? Most titles that managers have are well understood. Production Managers, Accountants, Administration or Personnel Managers seldom have to explain what they do and of what value it is to the firm.

Marketing itself is often confused with advertising or market research, or is used as a more fashionable term for selling.

Some professionals such as solicitors, dentists and architects see marketing as synonymous with techniques they are very nervous of even contemplating using, and which they perceive as being irrelevant, brash and likely to alienate the very people who will keep their businesses alive – the customers.

For the entrepreneur, it is essential to get a clear picture of what marketing is, how it fits in with running a business and how to do it.

Not one definition but three

The marketing professions have perhaps done little to clarify the confusion, since they use the word 'marketing' in the following three different ways:

Marketing is 'a concept'. By viewing a business through the eyes of the customers, the continued prosperity of a firm can be ensured by providing the customers with 'value satisfactions' at a profit, satisfying their needs rather than simply selling what the firm has to offer.

Marketing is 'a function'. Marketing is the total management function that coordinates the above approach, anticipating the demands of the customers, identifying and satisfying their needs by the provision of the right products or services at the right price, time and place. In other words, marketing does not just happen, someone must 'wear the marketing hat'.

Marketing is 'a series of techniques'. These techniques make the process possible. They include market research, pricing strategies, product development, distribution management and communication with the market and others, discussed throughout the book.

Let us look at each of these definitions in turn.

Marketing is a concept – Understanding consumer needs

No business can survive long if the goods or services it produces are not bought in the volume and at the prices that will cover the costs of borrowing money to buy plant and equipment, and pay salaries and suppliers.

It was believed that one way of solving this problem was to sell your goods more cheaply than any competitor. Although a breakthrough in manufacturing technology or access to low cost labour can give you such an advantage for a short time, it is not long before your competitors find out how to match your prices. Similarly, at the end of a price war, manufacturers often find that neither they nor their competitors have gained. All that has happened is that everyone is earning less profit!

A second approach is to use pressure-selling tactics, promising anything simply to secure an order. There has been a long series of disasters among British firms who followed this approach. Predictably, most of these are now out of business.

Modern marketing takes a different view of how to develop a healthy business. This point is, perhaps, summed up best by Peter Drucker's phrase 'the purpose of a business is to make and hold a customer'.* The logic of the case for modern marketing thinking can be seen as follows:

- People choose goods and services that best meet their needs. They may be poor at understanding what those needs are and how to make the right decisions, but they are still trying to satisfy their needs and solve their problems when spending their money. Entrepreneurs must understand their needs.
- If you can understand these problems and needs better than your competitors, you are well placed to design products or services which meet these needs and help to solve these problems better. However, you must be able to do this at a

---

* P Drucker, *The Practice of Management* (Heinemann) 1968.

profit. Which means you must understand what your customers are willing to pay.

- As society changes, new problems and new needs emerge which existing products and services are less capable of solving. The old products and services are threatened, and so are the firms who stick with them. Most changes in society therefore represent an opportunity for new products and new firms. Those entrepreneurs who can correctly read the signs, identify these needs, and develop and deliver new products or services will grow. Those who miss opportunities will stagnate or decay.
- The market orientation of the firm needs to be constantly checked. Unless everyone in the firm understands that the customer eventually pays the wages and decides whether there is a job, the firm will lose touch with its market, lose its cutting edge and begin to decay.

Example 1. Reading social change

Most office staff, and their numbers are growing, have a common niggling problem – how to find a reasonable lunch at midday. For the thrifty, it is solved by bringing their own sandwiches and eating at their desks. Those who do not leave themselves enough time in the morning to prepare their own lunch, seek out a sandwich bar or cafe. These have become so crowded in many towns that the pubs, seeing the opportunity, have entered the market in a substantial way, offering a congenial atmosphere and a low cost meal. Female staff, however, who want to use their lunch hour for shopping rather than drinking, responded to a third alternative. Entrepreneurs who do not want to burden themselves with the high overheads of a main street establishment and compete directly with the cafes and pubs, go directly to the offices, take the orders for sandwiches in the morning and deliver all the packed lunches at midday. Since they only need to make to order, they can guarantee really fresh sandwiches, or even hot meals. They can also provide truly vegetarian meals and cash in on a major trend in dietary change.

Customers' problems and needs are constantly changing in response to other fluctuations in society, such as alterations in its:

- laws
- economy
- values
- population structure
- technology.

Any and all of these may represent a new business opportunity. Those who wish to benefit from it, and are able to move in before others, are well placed to establish a good business for themselves and grow.

If you really want to design a product or service correctly, you need to understand that in a modern society, the needs you are satisfying are not simply the basic biological drives of hunger, thirst, shelter and sex. Psychological drives also have a role. Thus, a factory manager buying a machine needs to be assured that not simply the price, performance and delivery are competitive, since many other products are technically comparable. He generally needs to be assured that you can also satisfy his psychological needs, such as:

- Can I trust this firm to give me good service after the machine is installed?
- How can I justify my choice to my colleagues?

A successful marketer perceives all needs as existing in two dimensions. He understands the objective criteria the customer will use in choosing the product, such as:

- price
- measurable performance
- delivery
- installation costs.

He has also worked out the customers' psychological needs and built their satisfaction into the product design and total offering. It is often a better understanding of these subjective or psychological needs that enables you to make your product stand out from the alternatives, which are similar in other ways. This can only be done by treating your customers' problems as if they were your own. If you can really understand their worries and fears, you are a long way along the road to finding a better answer for them.

Example 2. Understanding psychological need to develop your business concept

Joan is a trained art historian with several years' experience in the business of purchasing, displaying and preserving fine paintings. She saw an opportunity to use her skills during the growth of new finance houses in the City of London and in Docklands. Furnishing offices for senior management and new boardrooms pose particular problems.

In financial institutions, the tone of the corporation is paramount. It has to project a strong image of being a trustworthy firm with ample financial resources. The decor is thus very important and quality paintings, well chosen, hung and illuminated, can play a major part in the process.

Seen from the customers' point of view, choosing the right picture is difficult enough since:

- directors of financial institutions may not have the best taste and may not agree among themselves which painting to choose;
- shareholders might object to extravagant use of company funds if the pictures chosen will not appreciate in value;
- the total effect is difficult to envisage unless it is understood what can be achieved by different lighting, positioning or a change of frame;
- for the picture to retain its value, it needs to be regularly inspected, cleaned and, if necessary, reframed.

Since Joan can provide a total service for her customers, her firm is successful because it provides:

- peace of mind that an expert who knows which pictures are coming up for sale can operate on their behalf and obtain them at reasonable prices;
- avoidance of friction between colleagues as to what is and is not good taste;
- satisfaction that the investment in art will appreciate in value and, in some small way, the firm will become known as an art patron.

Marketing as a concept – Matching company strengths to market opportunities

The competitive advantage

Understanding consumers and evaluating how well the available range of products and services meet their needs is the starting point for spotting business opportunities. Some gain such an insight by having been in the position of a prospective consumer themselves and experiencing the inadequacy of existing products or arrangements at first hand. For example, anyone who has tried to buy or sell a house and encountered the lethargy of certain estate agents can understand why property location agents are springing up so fast.

The habit of thinking like a customer, although it will illuminate opportunities, is not, however, the total process. In a competitive situation, those companies who possess the strengths that have most impact on their particular market will be the most successful. Thus, although all computer companies apear to have mastered information technology, the world leader, IBM, seem to have developed a consummate skill in setting industry standards, which all others then endeavour to meet. IBM have repeated this feat again and again, and this is what establishes them as a market leader and the other firms as followers.

A firm that has selected an opportunity that corresponds to one of its strengths starts off, therefore, with a competitive advantage which will increase the likelihood of its success. Hence the formula:

Growth opportunity + Company strength = Competitive advantage

All firms, therefore, need to clearly understand the nature of whatever company strength they possess, if they are to apply it to the right opportunity.

The sources of competitive advantage
Company strengths only affect success if they are brought to bear.

Example 3. Distinctive company strengths and their potential for competitive advantage

Company strengths . . .	can become a competitive advantage if:
Cheerful, helpful staff	Competition is using unqualified staff to cut prices (as, for example, in the travel agency business)
Speedy delivery	Customers have emergencies, price becomes a secondary consideration – this is the secret of the 7 to eleven chains where shopping is much faster than at a supermarket if only a few items are to be bought
Low cost production facilities	The customer decides the specification and is happy with a standard product (as in the manufacture of piece parts)
Technical know-how	Customers can save costs and also receive more than just a low price service (also in the manufacture of piece parts).

Strangely enough, a small firm operating in a market dominated by bigger firms, often unbeknown to itself, possesses a whole battery of advantages that can be used as the main plank in its customer appeal.

Example 4. The typical advantages of a small firm in the manufacturing, construction or service industries

Advantage to the customer	Source of benefit
Quicker response to customer needs	It has not committed all its capacity in long production runs/big orders
Personal service/closer relationship	It does not have a large number of customers, so each one can be individually served
Speedier, easier progress chasing	As it is small, there is less bureaucracy in order handling

Key company strengths of this sort must, however, be well founded. Identification of any vulnerable areas in your own firm can enable you to do something to prevent competitive attack. If you can identify such weaknesses in your competitors, you have identified an opportunity of taking business from them, and they will find it very difficult to prevent you from doing so.

Example 5. Vulnerable, distinctive competitive advantages

Company strength . . .	can become a weakness if:
Customers use the firm because of its location (eg, a corner shop)	Any competitor setting up close by can take business away
Family/personal relationships with an important buyer	The buyer leaves/dies

Distinctive competitive advantages can only become competitive advantages when:

- they relate to real market needs;
- some of these needs are not being met by your competitors as well as you could if you were to bring your company strength to bear;
- they are based upon marketing skills.

Marketing as a concept – Segmenting your market to direct your efforts

It comes as a surprise to many entrepreneurs to find that customers not only see the product or service in very different terms from themselves, but that different groups of customers have different criteria by which they judge products. For a given market, therefore, it is unusual for one product to be equally acceptable to all these different customers. Marketeers who want to understand their markets need to understand who these different groups are and how their needs differ from one group to another. Such groups are called 'market segments'. Dividing up the market into these groups is the process of market segmentation.

A moment's reflection on the car industry will illustrate this point. Although economists talk about car sales and the car industry as if it were a homogeneous market, when developing new models, marketers have to be very sensitive to the fact that different groups of buyers – that is, market segments – need very different types of cars, eg:

- Luxury cars are not engineered to meet a target price but are designed, on the contrary, to exhibit the financial or social success of their owners.
- Family cars represent a much bigger volume of sales and manufacturers can, therefore, use mass production methods to achieve enough space, fuel economy and comfort to meet the family's needs at a price it can afford. This is, however, the most competitive part of the market where profit margins are slimmest.
- The sports car has to meet the requirements of a quite different market segment and provide quite different satisfactions. Models that are successful in this segment are judged by their acceleration, racy looks and image. All these features are enhanced by their success on the race track.
- The low price segment of the market demands a car with still different characteristics. Since the buyer is unable or unwilling to pay anything but the lowest price, he will accept reduced comfort, performance and space in order to achieve that goal. Manufacturers realise that the only way these needs can be met is by a very basic car.

Astute car manufacturers thus produce the same model in two versions: a de luxe version for the higher price segment and a more basic version for the down-market buyer. With a small number of models, they can thus cover a wide spectrum of customers.

Most markets segment in this way. Even basic products such as sand, sugar or salt are used by different groups of consumers for different purposes and are available in different forms. As an example, consider the availability of sand:

- Builders' sand is available by the cubic metre and is dumped from a delivery truck.
- Small quantities of sand are available for the handyman from DIY stores in 5-kg bags or ready mixed with dry cement.
- Specialist sands for aquaria and gardening enthusiasts are similarly available in bagged form from specialist outlets.

The different groups of users appreciate the convenience of the different forms of packaging and accordingly are willing to pay more per cubic metre for the packaged form. If you can identify market segments whose needs are not catered for by the standard form of product, you may thus have revealed new profit opportunities or, for the new entrepreneur, the opportunity for launching a completely new business.

One market segment or several?

In considering any market and choosing the segments, however, a small entrepreneur may find that he is trying to meet conflicting demands from different segments and achieving respectable market standing in none. By thinking through the needs of the different market segments and taking account of the company's strengths, the entrepreneur is able to choose one or more segments on which to concentrate his efforts, and thus become a force to be reckoned with within the chosen growth segment.

Example 6. Segmentation

Most plumbing contractors who try to cover all types of plumbing work end up by disappointing customers. They may have to charge higher rates than expected, or become involved in unacceptable delays by having to leave a job half-finished to deal with someone else's emergency.

Successful plumbers are beginning to realise that the different segments of the plumbing market put conflicting claims on their time. They tend to achieve better profits and customer loyalty if they specialise in one segment and gear up to do it well. Among the segments into which plumbing contractors seem to be settling are:

- The emergency plumber: Several organisations concentrate on handling emergencies only. They employ independent craftsmen on standby and charge a premium price, but guarantee a 24-hour, swift service.

- The specialist bathroom fitter: Luxury bathrooms can cost several thousands of pounds and the enjoyment of such a bathroom can be spoiled by plumbers skimping the job. Specialist plumbers, on the other hand, working in close liaison with architects and show-rooms, know they can charge higher fees for better workmanship where quality is all-important.
- The plumbing contractor: This type of plumber has developed his business to a size where he can competently take on the larger contract, such as a housing development. Since he normally has to invest in plant and equipment, his costs are higher than the jobbing plumber and he would be unwise to try to compete for the smaller job. However, he often finds difficulties in competing against the smaller plumber on the smaller house renovation or housing association development.
- The jobbing plumber: This type of plumber is set up to handle a wide variety of small jobs. He loses the loyalty of his customers, however, if he is tempted to involve himself in any of the other three types of work. Unfortunately, if he is to graduate to one of the other categories, he does have to risk losing his present customers during the transition period, and unless he is very careful his reputation also suffers.

Those firms who wish to maintain their presence in more than one segment of their market may run into severe difficulties and may need to develop a very different package or offering for each segment, if their resources are not to become overstretched.

Example 7. Serving two segments of a market

A young electronics engineer, noting the increase in burglaries, rightly anticipated rising demand for burglar alarms. He therefore considered how he could best enter the burglar alarm market. Several substantial manufacturers were, however, already well established. Since their prices seemed rather high, he rightly spotted the need for a simple standardised, low cost alarm which DIY enthusiasts could fit themselves.

His first venture was, therefore, to sell the alarm by mail order, by advertising in DIY magazines, and in this he has been moderately successful.

Now, however, a new segment is opening up. As his alarms have become better known, he is receiving a substantial number of enquiries for a simple, low cost alarm. The enquirers, however, are not DIY enthusiasts, and therefore want someone else to install it. Our young friend now has to make some important decisions as regards his business.

- Should he develop his own installation service? If he does, is he risking competing against electrical contractors who might fit his alarms for their customers? If he competes against them, however, they might well advise customers to buy a rival alarm.
- Should he work with and through contractors even though this means giving them business he could keep for himself? If they install them badly, is he not risking complaints about his product which could harm his business?

His solution was to try to use his strengths, which lie in installation design, and work around his weaknesses, which are lack of funds to employ his own electrical installation staff. His strategy is therefore:

- In the area within a radius of 15 miles of his workshop, he will provide a complete service. This enables him to keep in touch with the problems of difficult installations.
- Outside this area, he will appoint a network of accredited electrical contractors whose work he will monitor and he will be able to handle the customer contact direct.

Most businesses have to choose the segments of the market in which they will operate. It is often the care with which they choose the segments that determines the future success of the business. Choosing a segment entails gathering information about that segment, its future potential, the strength of the competition and the company strength you will bring to bear.

Marketing as a function

Understanding your market enables you to choose your target market segments. Thus, you have a clear idea of:

- the kind of people you wish to serve as customers;
- the full nature of the need you are trying to satisfy;
- what customers are looking for in your product or service;

Now you know what you are trying to achieve, the second part of the process can begin: planning each element of the total range of activities by which you will serve your target audience better than your competitors do. Let us consider each element in turn.

The product decision

Now you understand what your target customer is looking for, you can decide upon the nature of the product or service you will offer in terms of:

- The 'quality' you will achieve. Offering a luxury product to a market segment whose main consideration is low price is inappropriate. Offering the second rate to a market segment which needs or is looking for high quality can be similarly disastrous.

- The 'completeness' of the range. Which extra services or extra components will they welcome you providing? Which will they provide for themselves? Should you include the extras in the total package or sell them separately?

The price decision

The quality and product range you choose will determine the cost of the product and influence the price. At the same time, the nature of the needs, which may be emergency breakdown service, will determine whether customers are willing to pay high prices for a modified form of the same service.

Unless you can understand what constitutes quality in the eyes of your target market, you are likely to get your prices too high or too low.

The distribution decision

In competitive markets, customers do not expect to go out of their way to find your products. If your product is not available at the right place or time, customers will take a competitive product or service, and you will continually lose sales.

If you know the buying habits of your target market, ie, where they look for your type of services or goods, you can ensure that your goods or services are available there. This is not always as easy as it seems. Although the obvious channel for your product may be, say, via DIY stores or chemists, every other manfacturer is competing to get their goods on to the retailers' shelves. You may well have to devise an alternative means of making your goods available. If you are offering a service such as hairdressing, the costs of renting a salon in the high street may cripple your business, and so other ways of getting the service to the customer may have to be devised, such as visiting their homes or offices, or locating in a less expensive area.

The sales promotion and personal selling decision

In your busy personal and business life, you do not always have the time or the energy to go hunting for better products or services. You expect manufacturers to tell you about their products and services via advertising and other forms of promotion.

This is not easy to achieve, however, since the lives of most people are filled with conflicting advertising messages; and so it is often difficult to be heard above the hubbub. But if you know what newspapers and magazines your target audience uses, you can at least beam your messages along the right channels. If you know what type of message and tone is acceptable to your audience, you are less likely to meet rejection.

The concept of the marketing mix

The four elements of marketing just discussed namely, product, price, place (where the goods are available) and presentation – are known collectively as the marketing mix and are all subtly interdependent. For example, the quality of the product generally determines its cost. If you want to increase the quality, you normally need, therefore, to increase your costs and prices.

A better quality distribution service normally means higher distribution costs. Persuading up-market retailers or distributors to stock your products generally means giving them larger discounts on the retail price.

Unless sufficient money is devoted to making your product known, customers will not appreciate what the product is, why it is good value or where it can be obtained. The price must, therefore, cover the cost of advertising.

All these costs, in addition to a reasonable profit, have to be covered by the prices you charge. Yet the price must be acceptable to the end customer. The problem of these interrelationships becomes almost too complicated to solve.

The marketing principle of starting your analysis by a consideration of the customers and their needs and developing a better means of serving them can provide a clearer guide. If you have a clear picture of the customers and their situations, the planning process can start.

● What is the nature of the needs?
● What is the importance of these needs in the lives and careers of your target audience?
● How satisfied are they with the present means of satisfying these needs?
● What are their buying and media habits?

You can now design a balance between:

● the product design and quality which the customer is most likely to accept;

- the price the customer will be willing to pay compared with others' offerings;
- the distribution method the customer will most appreciate;
- the message and media the customer will find most acceptable.

This balance or 'marketing mix' needs to be carefully designed. In the main, it is the creative orchestration of these factors that is the core of the marketing activity, upon which the business stands or falls in its efforts to provide satisfaction at a profit.

Checklist

- Read Example 1 again. Which changes in consumer habits have given rise to your business opportunity? What has brought about this change? How long will this influence last?
- What do your customers consider of value in what you are offering them? How does this compare with what your competitors are offering? How could you meet their needs better? What would such an improvement be worth to them?
- What psychological needs does your service or product offer? Put yourself into the shoes of your customers: What reason is there for them to believe they can trust you? Why should they think they can get on better dealing with you than with your competitors? If they have to justify choosing your product to others, what help do you give them?
- What is your competitive advantage? Is it a viable one or do you need to develop a strength? What competitive advantage do your competitors have? Do they use it against you? If not, what would happen to your business if they did? Do you use your competitive advantage to the full? If not, how would your business improve if you did?
- List your market segments: Identify the segments in which you are operating. Are you active in too many segments, trying to be all things to all men? Are you in too few and putting too many eggs into one basket? After re-reading Example 7, which segments should you concentrate your efforts on/deal with differently/move out of?

Part 2
The Internal Considerations

2
Understan
Market Dyn

In Chapter 1 you saw how, by understand your customers' point of view, you can segment your market, focus your efforts on areas of opportunity and use your company strengths to full advantage. This chapter develops that approach by, first, exploring a range of segmentation methods you could use and then introducing buyer behaviour models that can help you to focus your marketing efforts further. The more you understand your market, the better your marketing decisions are likely to be.

Segmentation criteria

In segmenting any market you are trying to define a group(s) of consumers who are of more interest to you than other groups. You are therefore trying to identify some character(s) or characteristic(s) that will distinguish it from the others. Such a characteristic is called a 'segmentation criterion'. There is, however, no one criterion that best segregates groups of consumers for all products at all times and for all purposes. Depending upon several factors, some criteria are more revealing and relevant than others. An astute marketer has, therefore, a wide choice of alternative criteria at his disposal so that he is able to choose the most appropriate for any given purpose.

In general terms, the most useful segmentation criteria meet three requirements:

- The criteria correspond to those used to prepare published statistics or to which you have access. If you can define the most prominent market for your business as 'jobbing printers within 30 miles of your office', it is fairly easy for you to identify how many of them exist and thus what your business prospects are.
- The criteria reveal a group of customers who are susceptible to unique marketing approaches because, for example, they

...ds from different outlets, read different advertis-
..., have different requirements in terms or products,
...ubstantially different quantities or are willing to pay
...erent prices. If the group is not unique, it cannot be usefully
considered as a separate category for marketing purposes. A
different treatment or approach would appeal to this group of
consumers. They will respond by placing more business with
the firm that catered to their specialist needs than with those
who do not.

- The criteria indicate that the business that can be generated is
big enough to justify producing a different service or product,
appointing different distributors or developing special advertising; that is, the return justifies the extra expense or trouble.

Segmenting consumer markets

The most common variables or criteria used for segmenting
consumer markets are as follows:

User status:	Where consumers form strong loyalties for
(a) User/non-user	a brand or supplier early on. This criterion
	can be very significant. Few people, for
	example, transfer their account to another
	bank, once they have opened a bank account.
	To attempt to get them to switch their
	account is, therefore, not as fruitful for the
	banks as focusing their efforts on those open-
	ing bank accounts for the first time, such as
	students etc. Tobacco manufacturers use this
	criterion to arrive at a different answer. The
	weight of their advertising has always been
	directed towards those who already smoke,
	attempting to persuade them to switch
	brands, rather than to persuade non-smokers
	to start smoking.
(b) Heavy/light	Heavy users of some products can be persua-
user	ded to buy in larger quantities, thus cutting
	selling and storage costs. Sometimes, on the
	other hand, they are aware of their buying
	power and can demand lower prices or extra
	services, and thus may not be the most
	attractive segment. A florist, for example,
	may identify local hotels as big potential
	users of cut flowers. But hotel managers

might prove to be very demanding, expecting high quality flowers, delivery and display, no matter what the season.

Purchase occasion   A gift such as a pen bought as a present is often better received if it is packed more lavishly. Similarly, glaziers who can offer a speedy window replacement service after a robbery find that they can ask and get a premium price for the service. They focus their advertising on the 'distressed' segment of the market.

Geographic   If the distance that can be covered is an important criterion or limiting factor, you may have to define your market as a geographical area. To work outside this area, you may need to develop a very different approach (see Chapter 1, Example 7).

Socio-economic   A family's income was once regarded as the most decisive factor in determining whether they would choose predominantly high quality or cheaper products. Skilled and semi-skilled workers, some of whose salaries have overtaken professional people and middle management, do not in the main, however, spend their money in the same way. They spend less on books, for instance, and more on such things as package holidays, fashion and beer. Thus, the concept of social status is a more useful criterion to distinguish one type of household from another, as illustrated in the National Readership Survey in Appendix 1. Since the number of each type of family is available for each district of the country, it is widely used as a criterion.

Demographic:
(a) Gender   Obviously, some products are only used by women while some are only used by men, and this criterion best defines the market for those products. There are some surprises, however. Men figure prominently among the agony column readers of women's magazines! Similarly, gender does define different behaviour. Women are very keen to celebrate

birthdays and other occasions by buying presents for relatives and friends. Astute marketers of cards and gifts thus focus their efforts on women as being the group who will best respond to their marketing efforts.

(b) Age group

Different age groups spend their money in very different ways. The success of a cinema relies largely on teenagers and young adults for their audiences. As senior citizens live longer, the demand for hearing aids, false teeth and sheltered accommodation is rising sharply. In areas with a high incidence of over 65s in the population, rest homes are rapidly springing up.

(c) Family life cycle

As a family goes through different stages in its life, it sets very different priorities in its spending patterns. Young couples setting up house are heavy spenders on furniture and beds and buy smaller houses or flats. If both partners are working, they may also spend heavily on cars and expensive holidays. As the first children arrive, wives often stop working completely. The family income suffers a setback and expenditure switches to children's clothes and food. As children grow up, the family spends more on teenage fashion, books and family holidays. As the children leave home, the family may move to a smaller house, refurbish the house or increase expenditure on hobbies. The final life stage is that of a retired couple or single survivor. Family income has decreased and a gradual shift towards expenditure on health and quieter activities takes place. For a large number of products and services, therefore, it is the type of family in their area which best describes their market potential. Northern Ireland, because it has a large proportion of young families in the population, represents one of the biggest potential areas for children's clothes, food and educational equipment in the UK in spite of its overall average family income being low.

A moment's reflection will indicate that if you want to pin-point the most interesting group of consumers to you, several segmentation criteria are often more useful than one.

Although 'user's status' may be the most revealing criterion, if you can identify which kind of person is predominantly a user and which is not, you can better visualise the type of person you are targeting. You can then identify their life style, their income and their interests, and in this way make your appeal more effective.

Example 8. Segmenting the beer market

In the beer market, there are four major product variants that meet most consumer tastes (Figure 2):

Consumer tastes	'Dry'	Bitter	Light lagers
	'Sweetish'	Mild beers/ stout	Bottled ales/ draught lager
		'Still'	'Fizzy'
		Physical characteristics	

Figure 2. *Major product variants of consumers in the beer market*

Although the total beer market is declining, lager sales are still increasing, which may be one reason why breweries give such emphasis to the marketing of this product and are so interested in those who drink it. Research indicates that draught lager is consumed principally by a group which can be described by two characteristics:

- Age: 18 to 25 years
- Sex: male.

Having identified who is the prime market segment, marketers carefully study the expectations this group has of the product in question. Further market research indicates that for this group, lager is part of a social event. An evening spent in a pub means that the product will be drunk in some quantity. The alcoholic content needs to be lower, therefore. Second, the product, given the tastes of this age group, needs a bland taste, and a fizzy consistency comparable to Cola is most acceptable. Since, due to its indeterminate taste, there is little brand preference, the product must be available in all bars if it is to succeed. The advertising is also finely tuned to this group showing young male togetherness and toughness. In this way, an undertanding of the market segment enables the manufacturer to produce a product, distribution and advertising strategy which closely fits what the market considers of value.

Segmenting commercial and industrial markets

If your customers are not individuals but organisations such as banks, offices, factories, shops or warehouses, a different set of segmentation criteria are appropriate, as shown by the following:

User status:

(a) User/non-user — All of these criteria may be highly significant
(b) Heavy/light user — in segmenting industrial organisations. Since so much more information is available on individual organisations as opposed to individual consumers, however, you can normally find a correlation between other criteria and use them to target your market.

Purchase occasion — These criteria are shown below.

Size of establishment — There are many instances where large firms use different equipment from small firms in the same industry or branch of commerce. Large farms, for example, can profitably use large tractors and other machinery which smaller establishments could not. Small industrial firms such as jobbing printers would favour suppliers who can provide small quantities of paper and other materials, since they do not have room to store large stocks of their own.

Technology of the establishment — The very different kinds of work carried out in an office as opposed to a coal mine might make the latter excellent prospects for heavy ventilation equipment and the former for air conditioning. In other instances, the difference in technology indicates the difference between heavy and light uses of certain products. Mineral extraction plants such as quarries represent only limited prospects for marketers of storage shelving, whereas toy manufacturers, who require large quantities of racking for storing the finished goods, may be able to consume 10 or 20 times as much of this product per establishment.

End use

Although certain establishments may be superficially similar in the work they perform, the type of use to which they put products often calls for a different type of product. Thus, a small publishing or design office may have completely different requirements for its copier than, for example, an insurance office. Similarly, certain other machinery may be subject to constant and heavy use in one type of establishment compared to another, and thus require a higher level of outside maintenance or spares. It may therefore be wiser to segregate these establishments according to the use to which they put their machinery.

Type of establishment

Government and local government departments sometimes have quite different buying procedures from private establishments and these may need different treatment. Supermarket groups similarly buy centrally and expect to deal direct with the manufacturer. Small corner shops normally buy supplies from a wholesaler and may thus need to be treated differently from either of the above.

When selling to this type of customer, a great deal of the work of classification has already been done for you. The standard industrial classification (which can be obtained from HMSO or a local reference library) classifies each industrial and commercial establishment; it is thus possible to obtain complete lists of all organisations in any given class, categorised by location and technology. Since the size of the establishment in terms of number of, say, personnel is also shown, it is comparatively simple to develop lists of names and addresses of firms according to any of the other criteria and thus concentrate your effort where it is most likely to bring results.

Buyer behaviour models

If you study the characteristics of your target group carefully, you may gain further insights into how to fashion your product, distribution, price and presentation more effectively. If you examine the pattern of their behaviour, you can also develop more appropriate methods of understanding and serving them. These patterns of behaviour or 'models' have been studied extensively by other marketers. If they are appropriate to your circumstances, you can benefit from some of the methods they have developed to gain a competitive advantage. Two such models are discussed here:
- the role model
- the buying task model.

The role model

If you examine the total process whereby a product or service is evaluated and bought, it is often apparent that both simple and complex purchasing processes pass through several phases and involve several people, each person playing a specific role(s). A simple case of a family purchasing breakfast cereals could be described according to the following roles each family member plays:

The process initiator. In most cases, it may be observed that the mother is the one who initiates the search for a packet of cereals, by checking before the family sets out for the supermarket whether more cereals are needed. A lot of advertising is thus aimed at the initiator for this and other products in terms of 'when next you are buying . . . '.

The process influencer. Children play a large part in the choice of brand of cereal and can often be seen putting their favourites into the supermarket trolley. Similarly, advertisers have picked up this role of children and advertise cereals direct to them, to take advantage of this influence.

The process decider. Mothers often override children's choice of brand on the grounds of nutrition or expense. Again, specific messages appeal to whoever carries out this role.

The buyer. Sometimes the decider and buyer are the same person. With husbands playing a greater part in the weekend shopping, the person who pays the bill is often the father and he may well need to be considered.

The user. If the person who uses the product has been overruled, he may make his feelings known whenever he uses the product, and the other group members may be persuaded to switch back to the user's choice on the next occasion.

How can an understanding of these roles help you to focus your marketing efforts?

The process initiator. Understanding *'who initiates the buying process'* helps sales people selling machines. Keeping in touch with customers' maintenance engineers, who cannot buy equipment themselves but can influence the customers' decision to repair or buy new equipment, gives the sales person advance warning of which machines are reaching the end of their existing lives. Thus, he can build up support for his product before the decision is taken to replace it.

The process influencer. They are often overlooked. For example, a photographer trying to break into the newspaper world may concentrate his efforts solely on the artwork directors. However, had he spent some time or effort on other relevant sectors in the newspaper office, such as the sports editor, he could well have been given an opportunity to produce work for the newspaper a lot earlier.

The process decider. In some situations it is not clear who decides, so you have to work through members of the group with lower authority. When you ask for an order, prevarication on the part of the contact can often tell you whether you are in touch with the decider or with those who will be most influential in the decision.

The buyer. Many commercial and industrial firms employ professional buyers. Their ability to buy without recourse to their colleagues is often limited to lower cost items or to negotiating the price after the group has decided on a shortlist of suppliers. The precise role of the buyer is often well worth careful scrutiny.

The user. It is often a wise strategy to include the user in the discussions, where he or she has a major influence on the decisions. In selling typewriters to offices, sales people are careful to ensure that secretaries know of any particular feature that makes their machine more attractive or can save them work. In selling tractors to farmers, wise sales people make sure that the tractor driver, as well as the farmer, is given a trial run during a demonstration and his needs are fully discussed.

In general, wherever group influences are at work, a wise marketer ensures that each member of the group is both identified and his particular needs and questions satisfied.

The buying task model

Many buying situations, both in consumer and industrial markets, involve a long-term relationship between the buyer and the seller. Marketers trying to break into such a market therefore encounter particular problems of changing consumers' habits.

There are three particular states of the buyer-seller relationship, as follows:

The new task. Where a consumer encounters a new problem that the product or service he normally uses does not solve, he may have to find a radically different solution. A farmer who has to take land out of agricultural production will often not know where to start in transforming it into use for leisure activities. A small entrepreneur who discovers that he cannot control his business accounts without using a microcomputer, but has never used one, may be in a similar situation. Marketers who wish to sell to this type of prospect must realise that the consumer needs a lot of information about how to define the problem, how to consider alternative methods and products or services, and reassurance that he has made the right choice. Heavy emphasis on low price or technical details may be self-defeating. This is the chance to build long-term relationships and they should be carefully nurtured.

The straight rebuy. Many organisations and individuals have suppliers they use both habitually and often. Thus, when they need to rebuy, the routine is usually straightforward. The price and delivery may be simply verified and an order issued. A wise supplier who has such customers will make the rebuy as easy as possible and, by implication, make it not worth his customers' while dealing with his competitors, since it incurs extra effort.

Wholesalers' sales force, for example, check retailers' stock for them and write out the order for replacements, so that the retailer has only to sign the order. A good dentist sends out cards to his clients every six months, proposing a date and time for an appointment to have their teeth checked, rather than leaving it to them to ring for a suitable appointment.

It is difficult for sellers to break into such a market. However, it is possible to do so by using the next approach discussed.

The modified rebuy. There are some buying situations where consumers contact several suppliers and consider their offerings in some detail. This routine is often followed when the decision is an important or difficult one. For example, when a family replaces the family car, several makes and car showrooms are generally considered, before a decision is taken. A firm that wishes to extend its premises may well put the work out to tender, even though it may use the same firm for small maintenance jobs.

In this kind of situation, the seller needs to adopt a different approach from those mentioned. The consumer may be convinced that he knows what he wants, but often he is open to suggestions as to how this may be better achieved. An astute contractor thus seeks to open up the discussion before he makes a bid without going back to the basic issues involved in the 'new task' situation.

The modified rebuy approach is also particularly appropriate to the seller who is attempting to break into a market made up of consumers who are in a 'straight rebuy' relationship to his competitor. A useful approach for the seller to adopt is to persuade his prospective customers to reconsider what they are trying to do, and thus to gain a hearing for his case. This can be a particularly telling argument when a prospective customer has been using the same services for some time, even though his own circumstances may have changed considerably over the period. A firm may have grown considerably in size and so may its consumption of, for example, office materials. Its supplier may not, however, have improved its prices or service, whereas a new supplier may well be able to persuade the customer to reconsider whether it should go on accepting slow deliveries or a poor selection. The new supplier is using a 'modified rebuy' approach. If the new supplier is wise, he will use all the strategies of 'straight rebuy', after he has succeeded in persuading the customer to switch to him, to ensure he does not lose this new customer to another 'modified rebuy' competitor.

Checklist

- If you are selling to consumer markets, which criteria are you using to identify who you are selling to?
- Should you reconsider these criteria to see if they meet the three conditions outlined at the beginning of the chapter – published statistics, customer susceptibility to different marketing approaches, the business is big enough to warrant a different approach?
- Which approaches could you use – a different message in your appeal, different product or service, different package, making your product available at times or places that are not currently possible, different prices?
- If you are selling to industrial or commercial markets, how have you grouped the different types of establishment? If they have different consumption patterns, should you differentiate your approach to these different groups? Should you give all groups equal attention or do some deserve more?
- Who are the different types of participants in the total buying decisions which involve your products? With how many of them are you in touch? What should you do to ensure that each is contacted by you?
- Which type of buyer-seller relationship predominates in your market? Are you using the most appropriate approach? When will you change your approach?

3
Researching the Market

The need for research

From the preceding chapters, it will be clear that successful marketing depends on your having good information on what is going on in the outside world and how it will affect your firm. In specific terms, you may need information on:

Future opportunities
- The size of markets you could enter
- The kind of competition you will encounter
- The degree of customer satisfaction with currently available products
- Distribution channels available.

New products
- Product and brand development
- Test marketing.

Present operations
- Measurement of market share and size of market
- Changes that can affect your business – competitive activity, government action
- Information on new customers, location, purchases etc
- Information on new distributors.

Media research
- Success or otherwise of advertising campaigns
- Cost and effectiveness of various media.

The flow of data

In running your business, you are constantly coming across scraps of information about the external world from all kinds of sources, as illustrated in Figure 3.

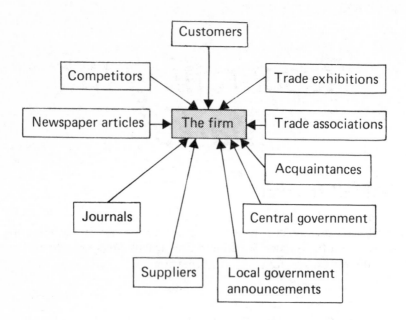

Figure 3. *Sources of information*

The purpose of market research is, therefore, to organise these flows into a system whereby you:

* gain advance warning of problems or opportunities;
* know where to get information when you have to take specific decisions;
* monitor your progress towards your business goals.

Big firms employ large numbers of specialist staff or outside agencies to supply them with this information. A smaller organisation, on the other hand, often does not have the same resources. However, it has the same business risks and, if anything, needs to be more efficient in going about the task of researching the markets than its bigger rival.

This implies that the manager of a small business must be able to master three important skills:

* He must be able to identify exactly what he needs to know and concentrate on what is important.
* He must follow a logical sequence.
* He must use sources of information that are not conditional upon having large resources.

The market research sequence

Well-organised market research follows a clear sequence:

- The problems are identified.
- The problems are clarified and the questions to be answered are formulated.
- The sources of information are identified.
- The data is collected.
- The data is analysed and put to use.

Let us consider these stages in sequence.

The problems are identified

Market research is not an end in itself but simply provides information from which action will result. If you are spending time gathering information that cannot lead to action, you should seriously question whether you should be spending your time in this way at all.

Further, it helps focus the research if you know the criteria under which you *will* take action. For example, if you were contemplating setting up a children's party service in your area, you would be foolish if you did not explore the market first.

What, however, does 'explore the market' mean? If you discover there are several families who could be interested, you have not really answered the question, which is whether you could make enough profit to make it worth your while giving up your present job and going into the business full time. The problem is now much more precise, involving questions about the cost of running a party, the price they would pay and how many parties you would be able to book in a year. You then need to compare the result with your present income and thus arrive at a rational decision based on facts.

You must not forget that market research can only provide information about the present and the past. It cannot tell you what the future will be. Nothing can do that! What market research can do, however, is to pin-point trends and show you what, all things considered, the future is most likely to be.

Similarly, it often cannot provide you with exact information. If you are examining a sample of the total population, the result is an 'estimate', never an exact quantification.

Finally, market research can only deal with problems that can be solved by the supply of information, which is why the first stage is concerned with formulating the problem, in terms of a question or strings of questions.

The problems are clarified and the questions to be answered are formulated

Clarification of a problem means turning a given problem into a series of questions to which answers can be found. This is not easy and one of the most important skills of the market research specialist lies in structuring the problem in this way.

Talking to others in the area of business or customers often helps to clarify what it is you want to know. These informal discussions give insights which are of immense value, as illustrated by the following:

- Do different types of people have very dissimilar needs?
- What different kinds of people are they?
- How do their needs differ?
- What attitudes do they exhibit to this problem?

Formulation of such questions frequently involves following a logical chain of thought. For example, if you want to know what profit margins are possible to achieve in a given market, you will need to find out:

- What price the customer will pay.
- What customers will expect for their money (the cost of providing it).

Similarly, if you want to know what profit you would make if you went into such a market, you will also need to find out:

- How many you will sell (number sold × profit margin).

The quantity you would sell would also depend on:

- How many customers you would attract from the total potential market (assuming some would not buy at all and some would place their business with a competitor).

Formulation of the questions generally means, therefore, translating one central question into several subsidiary questions.

Example 9. Estimating the size of a potential market for a new product/service

You want to estimate the size of a potential market for a new luxury product or an industrial service. Figures are unlikely to exist since the product does not itself exist. If you approached the problem by a series of questions, however, the answers, taken together, would add up to a full answer. You could then make a reasonable estimate. In this case, the series of questions might be:

- Who is the potential customer(s) – a particular social group for consumer products or a particular type of factory for the industrial service?
- How many are there? (As discussed below, the numbers in a given area can be ascertained.)
- How often do/will they buy this product or service?
- How much will they buy at a time?
- What price will they pay?

The answer to the original question is obtained by multiplying the answers to the last four questions together.

You could further develop information, which would lead to a total marketing plan, by asking additional questions on suitable distributors and advertising media:

- Which magazines and newspapers do they read?
- Where do they normally buy these goods?

The sources of information are identified

Information is derived from two major sources:

Primary data. Primary data is gathered directly from the people you are interested in for the purpose you have set. If you quiz retailers about the discounts they expect on the goods they handle and analyse the answers, you are producing primary data. Although it is very up-to-date information, it can take up a lot of your energy and time, which is why you always investigate first whether the information can be obtained by consulting secondary data sources, where all the work has been done for you by someone else.

Secondary data. Governments, associations and many other bodies are actively gathering and publishing data for their own reasons which are 'secondary' to your purpose. There is a wealth of such information available:

- in most public reference libraries;
- in trade or professional association libraries;
- in government libraries;
- directly from some of these sources.

A visit to any such establishment, a discussion of your needs with a librarian and a few hours spent reading through the information is an exciting experience. The most important sources are listed in Appendix 2. The type of information each provides and a suggested list of uses is also included.

Alternatively, you could combine both primary *and* secondary sources as illustrated in the following, which returns to the example of the assessment of a potential market for a new product/service.

Example 10. Assessment of a potential market using both primary and secondary information sources

- Who is the potential customer(s)?
  Primary: By showing a prototype of your new product to a selection of families, 80 per cent of AB social categories expressed interest; less than 30 per cent of the other categories did so.
- How many are there?
  Secondary: The AB class forms 17 per cent of the total population (see Appendix 1). This proportion is multiplied by the population of the area you will be covering to arrive at a population of 60,000 in your area.
- How often do they buy?
  Secondary/primary: Information on how often people buy this type of product on average may be prepared by such organisations as Mintel. The product may be so specialised, however, that primary data may have to be prepared while gathering information for the first question.
- How much will they buy?
  Secondary/Primary: Expenditures on groups of products may also be available from Mintel or Euromonitor.
- What price will they pay?
  Primary: If the product is very different or superior, this question may also be combined with the first question. A second insight may be gained from comparing the answer with the range of prices of similar products in supermarkets.
- Which advertising media do they read?
  Secondary: The National Readership Survey, among others, gives detailed figures of media use by different sections of the population.
- Where do they normally buy these goods?
  Secondary: ITV regional marketing handbooks give a complete analysis of the breakdown of purchases of each major type of product from each type of retail outlet.

The data is collected
After you have explored all the sources of secondary data, you can decide what primary data is required and how it is to be gathered.

There are several choices open to you as to how the data can be gathered, as follows:

- the research method
- the survey technique
- the questionnaire design
- the sample design.

Choosing the research method
Some studies try to gain a description of a market by identifying the characteristics of the customer, as in the preceding example. Others seek to identify what causes certain effects and calls for an experiment.

Much information can be gathered by 'observation', particularly if you have to answer questions relating to how much or how often, as illustrated by the following:

- counting the number of pedestrians who pass a high street store to determine the best location;
- counting the proportion of customers who stop in front of a new display cabinet to measure its impact;
- collecting the number plates of cars in a regional shopping centre or car park to determine from where the centre draws its customers;
- measuring the number of times certain books are borrowed from a library in a year to identify which type the library should buy more of;
- adding a time device to the cash register of a retail shop to measure the sales by the time of day and day of the week to see if it's worth keeping the shop open at certain times, such as Monday morning.

'Experiments' can be of several kinds and answer the question 'what if?', as illustrated by the following:

- offering the same product in different stores at different prices and measuring the effect on sales;
- testing different names of new products and asking for reactions;
- offering unlabelled samples of a new product and a competitive product to see if customers can detect any real difference between them.

The questionnaire or survey approach answers the question that neither of the other two approaches can answer; namely, why people behave the way they do. Let us deal with each in turn.

Choosing the survey method
The three types of survey are: personal, telephone and mail. A survey takes longer than observation, so once again, you should not proceed with a survey if you have enough information from the other approaches to solve your problem.

The 'personal interview' is a very popular survey method, since it enables the interviewer to interact with the people who are being interviewed, note their reactions and explore their motivations. Where general ideas are to be explored, a series of group or 'focus discussions' can help you to understand general feelings or attitudes on certain issues. A 'structured' survey, on the other hand, consists of a series of questions to which you seek answers either in business premises, for industrial or commercial products, or in homes or shopping precincts, to gain the views of consumers.

Alternatively, the 'telephone interview' is a very fast and inexpensive method of gathering information, since it dispenses with travelling time and costs. The method does have problems, however, since not every home has a telephone and, of course, it is not possible to see the visual reactions to the questions asked.

The 'postal survey', although the cheapest form of survey, suffers from real problems. It has to be clear and short, otherwise the questionnaires will not be completed and, overall, you can only rely on a certain proportion of people responding at all.

Finally, the 'panel' is a system normally used by professional market research organisations to measure changes in habits or attitudes over a given period.

Questionnaire design
Whatever the survey method, it is essential that you ask the same questions of all those you interview, so that the results can be collated and compared.

The phrasing of the question is therefore important. Questions need to be clear, unambiguous and user friendly if you are to obtain genuine information.

Questions can be of two types: 'structured' or 'unstructured'. Structured questions limit the respondents to a specific set of replies eg, 'Do you use gas, electricity or coal heating in this factory?' Structured questions can be multiple choice or simple checklist questions. Structured questions demand less skill on the part of the interviewer and are easy to analyse and collate.

Unstructured questions, however, give respondents more freedom to explain what they mean. However, problems of analysis may arise, since it is difficult to be sure whether answers given by different people using dissimilar words mean the same.

Questionnaire design is a complex art and readers are advised to consult the literature before undertaking a major project of their own.

Sample design

In cases where the total number of people you wish to interview is specialised and therefore limited, such as managers of fish processing plants, you can conceivably interview them all. Where the numbers exceed a hundred or so, you normally interview a sample only, which will then give an estimation of the way the total population behaves or thinks.

If you have or can obtain a complete list of 'the population' concerned, possibly from a telephone directory, a list of users or list of firms, you can take a random sample. Thus, from a list of random numbers produced for the purpose, you could interview a sufficient number of respondents, knowing that each has an equal chance of being chosen.

A simple form of random sample, the 'periodic sample', avoids this complexity. If your list of respondents numbers 2000, for example, and you wish to interview 100, you choose your sample by throwing a pair of dice or using some other mechanism to obtain a random number between 1 and 20. If 3 comes up, you then interview every third, twenty-third, forty-third etc name on the list until your 100 respondents have been chosen.

Random sampling takes several other more complex forms and reference should be made to the literature for further details.

In many cases, however, no such list of 'the population' exists. Where you have the breakdown of the population by different groups or types from secondary sources, you can construct a quota sample to ensure that you choose a sample in which each is represented by the correct proportion group in your sample. Thus, if you interview people at an exhibition hall or shopping mall, you can choose a sample that has the same balance as the total population you are examining. The table overleaf illustrates how such a sample is constructed.

The size of the sample you should take is another complex affair on which specialist literature can be of help. The larger the sample, the more accurate the results will be. However, as the sample size increases, so does the time, effort and expense, and a compromise has to be achieved.

Age	Percentage of total population	Number to be interviewed from each group
15–24	20	15
25–34	17	13
35–44	16	13
45–54	14	11
55–64	14	11
65+	19	14
Total	100	77

Table 1. *Construction of a quota sample*

The data is analysed and put to use

The most important decisions in the firm depend upon good market research information. Every effort should be made, therefore, to gather this information correctly. Particular problems to note are:

- Are your results distorted because they were true of only one time of year, or one geographical area?
- Did you really listen or observe or did you simply note those things that confirmed your prejudices?
- Did you really pay more attention to those who express themselves forcibly and neglect those who do not talk easily?
- Did you base your findings on those who were available for interview or replied to your mailed questionnaire and neglect the rest?

Market research, properly executed, will provide you with a wealth of information, some of it disquieting or disappointing. It is easy to reject information that does not conform to your views of yourself or your product. What is essential is that action is taken to exploit opportunities or avoid threats.

Appendix 3 provides a case study in the use of marketing research in the setting up of a retail business. Although the figures have been changed to preserve confidentiality, it is based on a real case for a real venture, which is at present very successful, due in no small part to the care with which the project was researched. An important lesson perhaps.

4
The Marketing Plan

'Planning is the organised thinking that precedes purposeful action.'

Why plan?

Some entrepreneurs get started in business by sheer chance or by just being in the right place at the right time. Sadly for them, it is difficult to keep a business healthy and growing by relying on luck alone. For a business to survive and prosper in a changing world, a better organised approach is needed.

A business cannot stand still. It has to develop new ways of serving existing customers. It has to seek out new opportunities and new customers, and to do that the direction in which the business should be heading and how it will get there need to be thought through.

Many find it useful to commit their ideas to paper in the form of a marketing plan since:

- writing their ideas down helps to clarify them;
- drawing up a programme of activities which is part of the plan helps to ensure that nothing is forgotten;
- it enables them to review progress and control the marketing operation;
- where external funds are being sought, financiers view a written plan as a sign of a well-organised business and a committed entrepreneur.

The marketing planning process

In essence, the marketing plan seeks to answer four important questions:

- What will you be selling?
- To whom will you be selling?

- How much will you be selling?
- At what price will you be selling?

The marketing plan arrives at the answers by following a logical sequence, as follows:

- The company mission: Where do you want the business to go?
- The external analysis: What opportunities and difficulties are in your path?
- The internal analysis: Which of your strengths and weaknesses will affect you getting there?
- The strategy goals: In which markets will you compete and on what basis?
- The marketing operations: What will be the role of each element of the marketing mix?
- Programming: How will you ensure that the necessary activities occur in the right sequence and at the right time?
- Budgeting: How much will the marketing operations cost?

The marketing plan is, therefore, using information about the present to shape the future.

Let us now examine each of these stages in sequence.

The company mission

The most successful entrepreneurs have a clear concept of the firm they are trying to build. For this vision to become a reality and the planning to start, you need to spell out both what you are trying to do and the constraints within which you wish to work. So, while the term 'mission statement' may seem just more imported American jargon, it has practical implications.

Example 11. Mission statement

This is how a professional woman expressed her business idea in a recent seminar:

'I worked for several years in the City of London as an accountant specialising in taxation. I have interrupted my career to start a family and have now moved to Hertfordshire, where I would like to set up my own practice.

'I would like to become a respected member of my profession and of my community. At present, I cannot work for more then five half-days per week but I hope, within five years, to have built up a client base of firms who are well respected in the community. From this base, I can start my own practice employing others at some future date.

'I do not wish to join another practice. I want to keep this business under my control and, if possible, have something to hand on to my children.'

A frank statement of this kind is invaluable for planning the market position of her business since it defines:

- the personal satisfactions she is seeking from the business;
- the geographical market in which she will operate (Hertfordshire);
- the type of client she is seeking and, by implication, the type she is not desirous of being associated with;
- the type of service she can offer (and is unable to offer);
- how fast she wishes the business to grow;
- by implication, what profits she will need to make to remain viable and independent.

During the next stage, she will explore whether this concept of the business will be realisable in the area she has designated. In this analysis, she may identify better opportunities. On the other hand, she may find that she needs to think through what she has to offer and, in the worst case, drop her plan altogether.

The external analysis

The indicators of environmental change
Chapter 1 described how changes in the environment can, on the one hand, bring new opportunities of doing business. On the other hand, environmental changes can cast severe doubt on the viability of existing ways of doing business.

These changes may take different forms. Demography, economic development or decline, social values and distribution channels may change slowly, so that you are often unaware of the change until it is too late to take action. Other changes, however, are more dramatic, such as government actions and legislative measures, technical breakthroughs and competitive action.

Since all these changes are outside your control, constant vigilance is required to evaluate the following:

- Will a given change have a long-term impact?
- Will it affect the survival or development of your firm?
- Will it change the competitive standing of your competitors?
- Will it allow you to compete where formerly you could not?

By examining seven common indicators of environmental change, a list of opportunities and problems can be developed for the Hertfordshire accountant to ponder.

Example 12. The analysis of the market for accountancy services in Hertfordshire

- *Demography:* As living in London becomes even more costly, young professional couples are settling in Hertfordshire and the other population is moving out.
  Opportunities: The newcomers may be seeking tax advice. As they are new to the area, they will not already be committed to an accountancy firm for this advice.
  Problems/threats: Some of the newcomers may themselves be accountants and so compete directly.
- *Government decision:* Stansted airport is to be developed on the Hertfordshire/Essex border.
  Opportunities: New firms will be attracted to the area who may require accountancy services.
  Problems/threats: Larger accountancy firms may well set up branches near Stansted.
- *Economic environment:* The economy is showing distinct signs of improvement.
  Opportunities: The first firms to benefit are likely to be small building contractors.
  Problems/threats: Once she gets involved in this business, the down market image may not be good for her firm. How can she turn them down without discouraging those she does want?
- *Social values:* There is a greater tendency towards self-employment by those who live in the area.
  Opportunities: There will be a sizeable proportion of people requiring basic tax advice. Some may represent good long-term prospects.
  Problems/threats: How can she find them? How can they be provided with low cost, standardised advice?
- *Legislation:* Accountants are now permitted most forms of advertising.
  Opportunities: For the first time in the history of the profession a newcomer can actively seek to attract clients and grow quickly.
  Problems/threats: The big partnership will already be using this facility and will have more funds than she has access to.
- *Distribution:* Banks and building societies, the traditional sources by which clients are referred to an accountant, are more active in helping the smaller business.
  Opportunities: Bank managers may be grateful for a wider choice of firms to which they can refer clients, especially if these firms have relevant, specialised expertise.
  Problems/threats: Banks are offering their own tax and financial consultancy services and could become her competitors.
- *Technological breakthrough:* With the widespread adoption of

microcomputers by business, accountants can offer their clients systems that are easier to use.

Opportunities: Not all accountants are conversant with the software and she will have a distinct advantage with her recent experience in the City.

Problems/threats: How will she convey her advantage over the competition without infringing the Accountants' Code of Practice?

The factual basis
The second stage of the analysis involves the gathering of the information that needs to be quantified in order to segment the market.

Example 13. The factual basis for accountancy services in Hertfordshire

An analytical sequence suitable for the accountant in Hertfordshire is as follows:

The structure of the market
● Which type of organisation needs accountancy services (by segment)
● How many of them are there in each segment?
● Which types of service do they use?
● How much do they spend per year?
Answers to these questions denote the 'relative size' of different segments.)

The attitudes in the market
● What do different market segments consider value?
● What do they think of the services they are using at present?
● What do they think of the accountancy firms they use?
● What makes them change their accountant?
● How often does it happen?
(Answers to these questions denote the vulnerability of segments to your marketing efforts.)

The competition
● Who are the competitors (direct/indirect)?
● Where are they?
● What fees do they charge?
● In which segments are they most strongly entrenched?
● How complacent are they?
● What range of services do they offer?
● How will they respond to competition?
(Answers to these questions show how you need to modify your assessment of the best market segments for you.)
● In which way is the market changing?
(This gives you a further chance to modify your choice of segment.)

The internal analysis

In this stage, you analyse the factors under your control and identify which are important for your success in this market. The factors you need to consider are:

- internal strengths/weaknesses
- external strengths/weaknesses.

A suitable analytical sequence is set out below. Some of these questions are more relevant to a firm that has been operating for some time. For the sake of completeness, however, the whole list has been included.

Internal strengths/weaknesses
- Do you have a unique product?
- Do you have a distinctive company strength?
- How are your facilities located in relation to the market you have targeted?
- Have you adequate financial resources?
- Are you set up to deliver a high quality or a low cost service?

External strengths/weaknesses

The client base
- Are you better at getting one type of customer as opposed to another?
- Are your customers in the growth area of the market?
- What proportion of their business have you serviced?
- How dependent are you on a small number of clients?

Range and quality of service
- How closely does your service and range of services reflect the needs of the market?
- How does your service range compare with that of your competitors?
- Is your range too narrow to satisfy the most attractive customer group?
- Is your range too broad to give coherence?

Price or fee structure
- Do you ask for and get better prices than your competitors?
- Does your pricing reflect the quality of your product?
- Do your clients perceive your prices as value for money?

Distributive strength
- If your business is dependent on outside bodies specifying your services or referring customers to you, have you created a relationship they wish to see continue and develop?
- How dependent are you on a small number of powerful distributors?
- Are you using the distributors who represent the best means of access to the markets you want to get at?

Promotion and selling
- To which market segment is your selling activity devoted?
- What do your customers know and feel about you?
- What proportion of your customers do you get through promotion?
- Are you using the right channels of communication?

It is not easy to assess the strengths and weaknesses of your own organisation objectively. By reflecting on each question in turn, however, you can arrive at a set of strengths, which should be exploited, and a set of handicaps, which will either need to be rectified or rendered less crucial by judicious choice of market segment.

At the end of the external and internal analysis, you will be able to summarise the strategic situation you face in the form of a chart – that is, the strengths and weaknesses, opportunities and threats (SWOT) chart.

Example 14. SWOT chart for accountancy services in Hertfordshire

Strengths
Unique tax advice competence. Good knowledge of software available for tax work makes her independent of requirement for large staff. Good references from previous clients. Price not difficult to justify in terms of savings in tax using computer modelling.

Weaknesses
Growth must be controlled so that business is not created which goes to a competitor. Needs to canvass new service organisations *before* they move, but not able to travel far with present family commitments.

Opportunities
Service organisations moving to area will not take to sleepy local accountants. The firms in this market have complicated tax problems which require a sophisticated approach.

Threats
Service organisations less dependent on locally based firms. Direct competition may move in at any time. Indirect competition from software houses. Two such firms are already exploring the possibilities.

From this, it will be seen that the accountant has a number of strengths which line up with at least one type of opportunity, but on the threats side several factors need careful monitoring. Several opportunities, on the other hand, have been rejected and one main one selected.

The marketing strategy
A marketing strategy consists of two elements:

- choosing the market segments in which you will compete;
- how to position your firm against competition.

Let us examine these two elements in turn.

Choosing the market segments
The market segments you choose to serve often determine, more than any other factor, the kind of firm you will become. The choice of segment is often more difficult for the small firm than the big firm, since often it cannot serve more than one segment without overreaching itself. The one segment it chooses, therefore, must be the right one.

Before choosing the segment, it is worthwhile finding answers to the following questions:

- Is there a niche in this market which has not been catered for?
- Is a large proportion of the consumers in this market satisfied with what they are being offered by the competition or are they looking for a change?
- Can you offer them something which really meets their needs?
- Will you generate enough business in this segment to survive?
- Is there too much business?
- Will you overreach yourself?
- Will competitors tolerate your entry because the market is growing? In a static market will they have to fight back, since you will be taking business from them?
- How long before they react? Will you be secure by then?
- Can you effectively communicate what you are offering?

Positioning your firm to meet the competition
If you have a clear picture of your target customers' needs and

your strengths *vis-à-vis* your competition, you can move to the next level of strategy development:

- How will you differentiate your offering from that of your competitor?
- Which elements of the marketing mix will you stress?

If you are selling services, it is difficult but crucial to differentiate your offering. Those who have succeeded in doing so have scored remarkable successes. This topic is illustrated in Example 15 and discussed further in Chapter 5.

Firms have found that concentrating on those elements of the marketing mix which are crucial for that *particular* market, and doing that *one* thing much better than their competitors, have given them the specific advantage which has produced their success. The elements of the marketing mix in question are:

- Product: The mix of products or services, the packaging of the product.
- Promotion: Making the offering more widely known, achieving firmer customer loyalty.
- Distribution: Giving the product or service better availability than the competitors' when availability is vital.
- Price: Gaining a better understanding of the value the customer attaches to the service or product offered.

Example 15. Differentiating a service – some examples

A good example of differentiation through concentration comes from the plant hire business. A building contractor in the middle of a building project whose bulldozer or grader breaks down is in a very difficult situation. The project may come to a halt and penalty clauses can cause substantial financial losses. Caterpillar Tractors understands this problem and has built its reputation largely on the excellent, worldwide distribution service for its spare parts. These can be rushed to any customer so that the machine has less down-time than the competition. Caterpillar equipment is thus first choice in the building industry and commands the highest prices.

All high street banks provide much the same services. Once a customer has opened an account, he or she seldom moves the account. The marketing problem for the bank is thus to make the bank different or special to the investor, hence the creation of the 'personification' of the bank by such images as 'the listening bank', 'the Black Horse bank', 'the friendly bank', simply to differentiate themselves to the prospective investor. Whether the banks should spend a little more time and effort improving their service to consumers and achieving real differentiation in customers' eyes is perhaps a matter they might spend a little time considering.

In the highly competitive, fast-food business, firms who provide basically the same hamburger also need to create differentiation for themselves. When consumers' perception of McDonald's quality slipped temporarily, Burger King exploited the 'flame broiling' concept in one campaign and Wendy's used the 'Where's the beef?' campaign to attempt to create a superior image with great success in North America.

To be second in the car hire business is not an easy situation to rectify. Avis Car Hire, for example, could not claim that their cars were better or safer or that their rates were lower than those of the market leader, Hertz. Instead, they made a virtue of necessity from not being the market leaders, saying 'We try harder!' a claim which Hertz could not counter.

A London plumber wanted to make a special appeal to his market. Several cowboy plumbers in the area had sent out unskilled workmen with disastrous results. He wished to communicate the idea that he was a local, friendly craftsman who did all his own work and guaranteed the standard. His used his first name, Ted, in the company name of 'Justed' to get this idea over. His business is thriving.

Defining marketing goals

You have now taken several decisions concerning what you are going to achieve in the market place. These objectives must now be translated into actual sales figures or targets. There are basically three stages to this operation:

- Identifying the sales potential of your chosen market.
- Deciding which market share best illustrates your long-term view of where you should stand in the market.
- Identifying which increases in sales performance each year are feasible so that your long-term objective is reached in a reasonable time.

Two examples will illustrate two different approaches.

Example 16.

An entrepreneur aims to become market leader in his particular area, which means that his market share will then be bigger than any competitor, the biggest of which has a 25 per cent share at present. The market has 900 potential customers who, on average, spend £550 on a particular service.

He sees his goals as follows:

Desired market share = 30%

Market potential $= 900 \times £550 = £495,000$
Desired sales, long term $= ^{30}/_{100} \times 495,500 = £148,500$

The marketing goals at present day prices are:

	No of customers	Sales	Percentage increase on previous year
Year 4	270	£148,000	22
Year 3	220	£121,000	47
Year 2	150	£82,500	100
Year 1	75	£41,250	0

The implications behind this analysis are that he believes it feasible to attract 70 new customers each year, and he can thus achieve his goal by the end of year 4. The percentage rate of increase in total sales will slow down, however, which is quite normal as the market becomes saturated. The sales goals he is now committed to achieve are feasible and, he believes, attainable.

Example 17.

Many businesses are slightly different. The external analysis may indicate that customers share their patronage between different suppliers. An entrepreneur has not had a full product line and so he could only obtain part of the business available. He has now put this right by introducing a full line of products and wants to calculate the effect.

If the average expenditure per customer on this line of products is £550 and his sales are £41,250 from 200 customers, then the average business he is getting from each customer is therefore:

$^{41,250}/_{200} = £206.25$

This represents only 37.5 per cent of the business the customers are placing.

If the new product only pushes his share up to 50 per cent of the customers' expenditure, his sales would be:

$^{50}/_{100} \times 200 \times £550 = £55,000$

This represents an increase of £13,750 per year. If this can be achieved over two years his goals are:

	Sales
Year 2	£55,000
Year 1	£48,125

Present Sales   £41,250

The question the entrepreneur will need to address is whether this increase is sufficient to meet his vision of the business he wishes to create or whether he should expand his market as well, as in Example 16.

The marketing operations

Now the goals have been set on a year-by-year basis, each element of the marketing mix can be assigned a specific role in bringing about what is to be achieved, as follows:

Product or service

- Is part of your product mix out of date and in need of replacement?
- When will a new replacement be required?
- Are some items of your product mix required so seldom that you could eliminate them and concentrate your efforts on those that have a future?
- Which of your products or services should be better packaged and what effect would this have on sales?
- Which new customers will you attract by a product developed especially for them?
- Do you sell across the range or only sell those products that are easy to sell?

Price

- To what extent does your price reflect quality?
- Can you raise prices and increase your return?
- How can you use differential pricing?
- Does your price give your distributors a fair return?
- Does your discount for quantity system need to be revised to increase sales or produce a better return?
- Can you use minimum order quantities?

Distribution

- To contact your targeted new customers, how many new distributors do you need to seek out, appoint and motivate?
- How many extra sales can you achieve by motivating your existing distributors better?
- If you get your business via specifiers or referrals (such as architects, bankers etc, how many more will you need to contact to achieve these extra sales? How will you persuade them to work with you?
- How much extra business would you get from your existing clients if you increased your delivery service or opened an office or warehouse near them?

Sales promotion and advertising
- To generate the number of new customers you need, how many enquiries will this represent and how much advertising effort will be necessary to create these enquiries?
- What new additions to the promotion mix do you need to attract the new customers (direct mail, exhibitions)?
- Do you need to be better known among these new customers and can PR help you?

Personal selling
- How many more sales calls will be required to generate the new business and how will you fit these into the rest of your work?
- How can you be more effective in getting orders so that you get increased business from the same sales effort?
- What would be the effect of better sales literature, samples and more adroit selling?
- Can you keep in touch with more customers by phone?
- Can you do more selling over the phone?
- How will you deal with more enquiries and orders?

Programming
In the previous section, the activities that will be necessary for you to reach your goals were identified. You can now synthesise them and identify:

- which activities need to be treated sequentially – for example, you normally have to appoint distributors *before* you can expect them to increase your sales;
- which can be treated in parallel – for example, you can book advertising space while you are working on advertising copy;
- working back from the date by which an activity should be completed, which are the latest starting dates for each activity;
- what is the work load involved (per week, per month) and how will this be fitted in with the other work you have to do.

These activities can then be entered on to a wall chart (and your diary) and regular checks initiated on each project to see if it is on schedule.

Budgeting and control
Before any plan is implemented, it needs to be costed – perhaps it is worthwhile to refer back to Chapter 3 again. After having thought through a plan and costed it, however, the costs may well exceed your financial ability. In such a case, the plan may have to

be reconsidered in order to find cheaper or more effective ways of achieving the same result. Finally, you need to set a budget to guard against overspending.

Control of the marketing operation is an important and complex task and Chapter 10 is devoted to the subject. For any plan to produce results, however, controls need to be inserted at the time the plan is developed. That is, the plan should identify the results you are expecting and when they should appear. If the expected results do not emerge, alternative action will need to be considered if the overall goals are to be met.

Planning is a habit

The marketing of a business is a key factor in its survival. If it is to be successfully managed, it needs to be carefully planned, the results you require identified, and the activities which will bring these results about thought through, organised and controlled. At the end of each period of the plan, a review needs to be made of the success achieved and how even better results could be achieved in the next period. In this way, you gain an increased understanding of the potential of your business, you gain in confidence, and you increase your power to compete and survive.

The habit of good planning is often a critical factor in the vigour and health of small firms.

Checklist

- Do you have a planning system? How would a written marketing plan assist you?
- What is the mission of your firm? Can you state it in terms that enable you to develop objectives and constraints?
- How will your geographical market be affected in the near future by demography, government decisions, economic environment, social values, legislation, distribution and technological breakthrough?
- Complete the factual base analysis in Example 13. What opportunities exist for increasing the accountants performance? What problems or threats will she have to overcome? How can she do this?
- Complete the internal analysis on page 62. What weaknesses does your firm have? How does this affect your ability to serve your target market compared with competitors? What action is necessary to turn them into strengths? What strengths have

you got which you can exploit? What has to be done to enable you to use them?

- Have you evaluated the different market segments open to you? Do you wish to change to another segment, combine another segment with the one you are directly operating in or further exploit the one you are in?
- How have you positioned your firm against competition? How can this positioning be improved?
- Have you defined your marketing objectives? Could they be defined more clearly? Should they be defined for a longer period ahead?
- Have you defined the task which each marketing activity has to perform so that each contributes to the achievement of the marketing objectives?
- Have you programmed the activities so that each activity is in the right sequence, the start date of each is clear and there is no overload of activities at any point?
- Do you budget and control your marketing activities? Do you learn from past successes and mistakes?

5
The Product Plan

Marketing and the product

As the preceding chapters have shown, a firm may survive and prosper only if its range of products or services, which have been called the firm's 'offering', meets the needs of the market segments targeted, at a price consumers are willing to pay. The choice of offering is, therefore, a crucial marketing decision. If you choose unwisely, it is unlikely that clever sales promotion, pricing or distribution will ever compensate for your mistake. Again, since potential customers judge your firm by the quality of your offering, once you have made an unfavourable or unfortunate impression, it is difficult, time consuming and costly to change their opinion of you. In the long term, mistakes about the product can be ruinous.

This chapter examines the question on two levels:

- How can you ensure that your present product range is viable and how can it be improved?
- Which new products do you need to develop to meet changing market conditions and how can you go about it?

Throughout this chapter, the term 'product' is used to denote a set of services or a set of tangible products marketed by your company, since the problems discussed apply with equal validity to both kinds of business.

Management of the product range

There are three analytical approaches that you can use:

- the three-level analysis of the product;
- the dimensions of the product range;
- development of a product range policy.

Let us consider each of these approaches in turn.

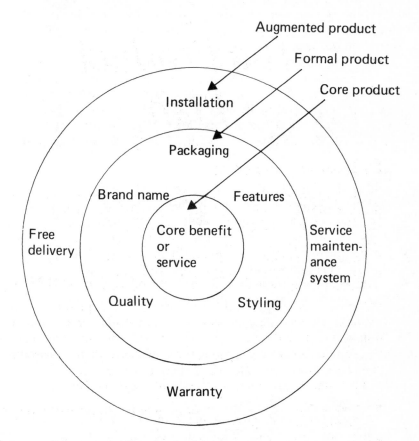

Figure 4. *Three levels of product*

The three-level analysis

You could gain a very useful insight into how your existing offering can be made more valuable to your customers if you could only look at what you are offering through their eyes. Research suggests that they do not judge your product or service in isolation. Instead, they see your offering as having differing dimensions or levels, as set out in Figure 4.

At the most 'basic' level, customers evaluate the core product or offering in terms of the benefit which ownership of the product will give them. The purchase of a camera, for example, can help some people relive memories. A camera provides an estate agent, on the other hand, with a quick means of making an attractive visual image of a property for sale.

Your first concern is, therefore, to evaluate whether your product meets these needs and whether it can be modified to perform this task better.

The 'second' level concerns the formal product itself, the actual service or product the customers are buying. For a physical product, some of these aspects are fairly easy to identify and evaluate against competition. For example, does the packaging of your product affect the quality inherent in the product or is it letting you down? Does the styling or the features you offer give you an advantage or disadvantage compared with your competitors?

The 'third' level is that of the augmented product and includes those added elements which help customers to enjoy the product after it has been bought and encourage them to come back to you when they are next in the market. An advantage over your competition at this level may well be the crucial difference between your offering and what the competitors are offering.

All elements of these three levels of the offering need to be constantly evaluated and re-evaluated to establish the following:

- Would an additional feature or service add value to your offering?
- Are there elements of your offering which are unnecessary in the eyes of your customers and should therefore be removed?

The marketing of services

If you are concerned with the marketing of services rather than products, it is even more important to consider whether you can gain an advantage over your competitors by developing levels 2 and 3 of your offering. Figure 5 illustrates the elements of the offering that an airline makes to its passengers. Long ago, marketers in this field learned to distinguish between the tangible and intangible elements of their offering. By improving and stressing the tangible elements, they have created an image which both attracts new customers and retains the existing clientele, often at little extra cost to themselves. Successful hoteliers have adopted a similar approach. A fresh apple and orange left on a bedside table cost very little but give a feeling of thoughtfulness and a welcoming attitude by the management.

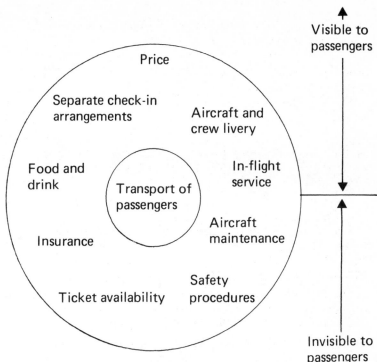

Figure 5. *The augmented product of a passenger airline*

Analysis of the product range

Some firms, such as Coca-Cola and Kentucky Fried Chicken, have achieved enormous growth on the basis of a very narrow product base. Similarly, a well-known UK firm has founded a business on one service, that of disinfecting office telephones!

There are many advantages in keeping the offering narrow:

- The firm can become well known by doing one thing, but doing that one thing well.
- The firm is less complex to manage with only one set of skills to master. Similarly, training of staff is so much easier if the range of operations they have to learn is limited.
- In some instances, the firm can buy raw materials in bulk or use high volume machinery to achieve economies of scale.

Other firms find that, unless they keep a full range of products, their customers go elsewhere to obtain the goods or services they do not offer. If they find they are happy dealing with the competitors, they often do not come back.

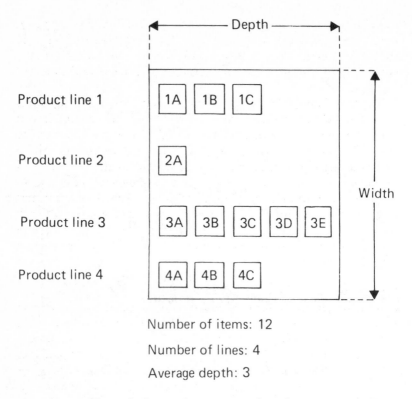

Number of items: 12

Number of lines: 4

Average depth: 3

Figure 6. *Conceptual representation of a product range*

Thus, estate agents find that, in addition to acting as arbitrator between purchaser and seller, they need to offer other services, such as mortgages, insurance, valuations etc, to encourage property sellers to come to them. Tool manufacturers, such as Stanley Tools, market a range of both DIY and gardening tools, since it believes that by meeting a wide range of its customers' needs, it does not lose them to competitors.

The product mix is thus a crucial decision area, the elements of which are shown in Figure 6. The product mix has three dimensions: width, depth and consistency.

The 'width' of a product mix describes the number of lines it markets; for example, hammers, rakes, chisels and spades constitute lines for a hardware manufacturer. By increasing the width of its range, a firm is implicitly capitalising on its good reputation and skills with its present customers.

The 'depth' of the product mix refers to the number of items in each line; for example, a line of hammers could include carpentry, metal working and sledge hammers. By increasing the depth of the product mix, a company hopes to attract as wide a spectrum of customers as possible, catering for different needs and different tastes.

The 'consistency' of the mix indicates how closely the products are related to each other both in terms of how the customers will use them and also whether the skills used to produce them are the same. Through increasing the consistency of its product mix, a firm is trying to create an image of excellence in a particular field of endeavour. Black & Decker, for example, have built up an enviable reputation as marketers of power-assisted tools, so that consumers contemplating buying a new type of power tool seek out the Black & Decker product first. This gives this firm a much greater chance of its product being selected and consequently a big advantage over its rivals.

Management of the product range policy

A new firm must be particularly careful in deciding its product range. When a firm is new, its potential customers are often trying to make sense of what it does or does not offer. If it is no different from the existing suppliers, there will be no great incentive to change. On the other hand, a firm that has no clear concept of its business may have great difficulties in creating loyalty among its clientele.

On an on-going basis, therefore, you need to examine and re-examine your product or service range, as follows:

● Have you included in your range those products or services which are more likely to be in demand in the future?

A firm of accountants, for example, although offering the normal services of auditing and tax advice, may have put little effort into developing computer-based acountancy facilities and financial packages, which are likely to replace many of the present services.

● Have you some product or service lines that have highly seasonal demand?

Services or products such as plumbing that are in great demand at one time of the year are often short of business at another time, such as during the summer months.

The introduction of a new service or product which would use the manpower or resources that are idle in the slack season can transform a business, particularly if this new addition is aimed at

Product	Sales	Percentage of total sales	Variable costs	Contribution to company profits	Percentage gross profitability
A	£84	44	£60	£24	29
B	£20	10	£10	£10	50
C	£25	13	£15	£10	40
D	£64	33	£38	£26	41
Totals	£193	100	£123	£70	100

Table 2. *Comparative profitability of a company's product range*

the customers with whom you are already in contact.

● How does the profitability of each product line compare?

Table 2 compares the comparative profitability or contribution of each of four products which make up a particular company's product range. The method of calculating the contribution of a product is discussed in Chapter 6.

An examination of the relative profitability of the four products shows that product B is by far the most profitable with a gross margin of 50 per cent. If extra efforts are devoted to increasing the sales of this product, the effect on profitability will be dramatic. For every extra £1 worth of sales of this product, the return will be almost double that of an extra £1 of sales from product A, which has a margin of only 29 per cent.

Product A, however, yields almost one-half of the company's sales and over one-third of its total profits. The company could not survive a sudden loss of this product's sales and contribution to profits. While this dependency lasts, it must hold on to its market share for product A while doing all it can to improve its sales of the other products.

The firm is also heavily dependent on the contribution and sales of product D, whose margin is also the second highest among all four products. All things being equal, this line should deserve the greatest push.

● How does the future potential for each product line compare?

It would be unwise on the basis of profitability alone to take the final decision as to which line should receive the maximum sales effort. The analysis should be continued further to take the market potential of each line into account, as shown in Table 2 above.

The development of new products

The development of new products is one of the most difficult tasks in marketing because:

- a product failure can represent a major set-back for a firm;
- many product ideas never become commercially successful. Recent research indicates that over 50 product ideas are necessary, on average, to produce one product that can be judged as a commercial success;
- imitation can be as profitable as innovation if rivals can launch a comparable product quickly;
- in areas governed by leglisation, governments and social groups are becoming very suspicious of new product ideas and may be very slow in giving permission for them to be marketed.

Since all customers expect you to provide them with a constant stream of new products and service concepts, all firms, if they are to survive, need to consider constantly how they will go about finding or developing new ideas on a continuing basis.

The process of finding and developing new products needs careful organisation, as follows:

- Assign the responsibility for the task.
- Generate ideas.
- Screen out those ideas that do not pass the business analysis test.
- Develop the product concept.
- Develop the brand concept.
- Test marketing.
- Full launch.

Assign the responsibility for the task

Since, statistically speaking, such a large proportion of ideas come to nothing, a large number of ideas will need to be generated to produce one worthwhile one. Therefore, unless someone within your firm takes on the task of developing new product or service ideas, it is very likely that none will emerge until a crisis point is reached, and competitors launch a product that really threatens your business. Similarly, a certain amount of that person's time and energies needs to be spent each period on searching out, evaluating and discussing ideas. Often in a small firm the owner takes this task upon himself. However, other successful entre-

Product	Market share	Competition	Market potential	Product strategy
A	50%	Two strong competitors	Mature market, little new growth	Maintain market share/profits; no new investments
B	30%	Several imitators	Growth market, to 12 times present size	Long-term investment: if market share maintained, B will replace A
C	20%	Distinct advantage over three competitors	Growth market, to three times present size	Prospect of aggressive strategy paying off
D	40%	Smaller, weaker competitors	Growth market, to double its present size	Maintain market share, concentrating on increasing profitability

Table 3. *Comparative market potential of a company's product range*

preneurs, while keeping the overall responsibility for this task in their own hands, have established good contacts with outside specialists or delegated it to one of their own staff.

Generate ideas
There are many sources and techniques available to you for generating ideas.

Outside sources
Typically, keeping track of other people's ideas can spark off new ideas of your own, eg.:

- patents filed in the Patent Office;
- technical magazines;
- exhibitions in which competitors and overseas manufacturers exhibit;
- customer suggestions, complaints and enquiries;
- suppliers' ideas;
- purchasing and dismantling of competitors' products.

Attribute listing
This technique involves a detailed examination of the attributes of existing products or services in turn, in order to determine how they can be improved or give better performance or greater appeal.

The humble screwdriver, for example, has been improved in many ways using this technique, as illustrated in the following table:

Screwdriver attributes	Possible improvements
Round shaft	Hexagonal shaft to take wrench to remove stubborn screws
Flattened blade	Pozidrive. Blade stops screwdriver slipping
Solid handle	A waste of space! A hollow handle can store spare screwdriver bits making it multi-purpose
Manual operation	Use power drive!
Torque obtained by twisting	Torque obtained by pushing, which stops the screw slipping

Improving existing products

There are many ways in which a consideration of existing products or services has produced better products and better services by:

- *Adapting*: A Japanese manufacturer of electric blankets posed the questions 'Why do we only have to make electric blankets that we can sleep on? Why not one that goes over the sleeper?' His new model made all others look second rate.
- *Modifying*: This approach produced the spade that turns the ground over for you!
- *Minifying*: The stereo became the Walkman.
- *Magnifying*: The mini became the maxi family saloon.
- *Substituting*: The expensive Gillette product was replaced by Bic's throw-away razor, creating a brand new business. Substituting stainless steel for normal steel produced a set of gardening tools that are easier to use in winter.
- *Rearranging*: This also gives rise to new ideas. Instead of using plastic bags simply to deliver compost to gardens, why not puncture the plastic and make a grow bag?
- *Combining*: Instead of providing separate compost and pots for seedlings, why not combine them into grow pots?

Brainstorming

This method involves a group of people meeting and setting themselves the specific task of developing a given number of ideas, no mater how outrageous, within a given time. The purpose is to suspend each person's critical facilities and record as quickly as possible whatever comes to mind. Many wild ideas, after suitable adaptation, can be modified into good product ideas.

Business analysis

Before time and money is invested in product development, a thorough business analysis needs to be undertaken to screen out those ideas which would never become financially viable. The process should include:

- Desk research to establish:
  the size and growth of the market, the level of competitive activity, and the importance of promotional activities.
- Field research to establish:
  if a prototype or drawing is available initially, so customer reactions can be tested to establish demand; reactions to

different levels of prices; and different variants necessary to
cover the market.
- Research to establish costs of:
producing, packaging, distributing the product, and additional
necessary capital.

Cash flows and break-even points are needed to establish at which
point the product will be profitable.

At the end of this process, each product idea can be ranked and
those that do not meet the profitability criteria dropped.

Develop the product concept
At the end of the screening process, you will have a list of possible
ideas that you can see yourself marketing. You need to develop
these ideas into product concepts, which include an image or subjective picture that your customers will form of the product.

As an example, a product idea could be that of a snack which
has an improved taste and is less fattening. There are many alternative concepts depending on three factors:

- Who will use it: infants, children, teenagers, young adults,
middle-aged adults, senior citizens
- Primary benefits: taste, energy, nutrition, refreshment
- Occasion when consumed: snack between meals, bar snack,
addition to packed lunch, substitute for a meal.

There are thus 96 different permutations from which the manufacturer will have to choose. Assume that he decides that the
greatest market scope is for a meal substitute for adults, since it
would best meet his own needs for:

- high sales;
- rounding out his present product line;
- using the production capacity he has available;
- greater profitability.

To develop the product concept the manufacturer needs to
identify how his product will relate to other forms of meal substi-
tutes open to his target consumer. By simple questioning, he is
able to identify that for most people there are two criteria which
are most important to them; namely, how substantial the snack is
and whether it is sweet or savoury. Consumers' perception of
these criteria can, of course, be measured and a 'map' created, as

illustrated in Figure 7. Each form of snack can thus be positioned on the map according to its taste and how substantial it seems. Figure 7 shows that pies are perceived as the most substantial snack and popcorn as the least substantial.

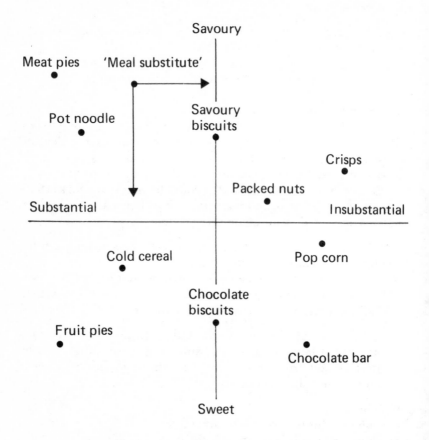

Figure 7. *Product positioning map (snack market)*

The new product, 'meal substitute', can now be positioned against its rivals. If, during the development process, it becomes 'less substantial', it will move closer to the segment of the market dominated by the powerful crisps and packed nuts manufacturers. Since their price bracket has been established for some time at a low level, and they have substantial resources, competing in this field may be a dangerous move.

If the development staff push the fledging product towards the sweet snack area, on the other hand, as shown by the vertical arrow, it may be difficult to justify the new product as less fattening.

The market positioning of a new product is crucial, therefore, and, although some leeway can be given to the development staff, a substantial shift of position may make it another technical triumph or a market flop.

Develop the brand concept

A further set of decisions needs to be taken in positioning your brand against other brands. In the case of the snack manufacturer, research indicates two major concerns:

- price
- calorific value.

Figure 8 on the following page locates each of the brands of meal substitute snacks available, against which the manufacturer will be competing, on a map that shows these criteria. From this map, it is clear that all three are designed to meet the needs of very different market segments.

These brands are not competing head-on; rather, each is operating in its own niche. The manufacturer now has to decide whether the low calories/low price segment is a large but neglected segment at position 1 or whether he should design his product to satisfy the broadest possible market of position 2, trying to be all things to all men. It is only when he has decided which market position he wants his product to take up that the product can be designed to meet the market needs at a price customers will pay.

The use of consumer tests

As an essential part of the development process, ideas need to be tested on a small representative group of consumers. For example:

- Can they open the packaging without spilling the contents?
- Can they read the directions? Can they understand them?
- Would they pick it out from a dealer's shelves?
- What do they associate the brand name with?
- Would they remember the name?
- What problems would your distributors have in selling or displaying it?

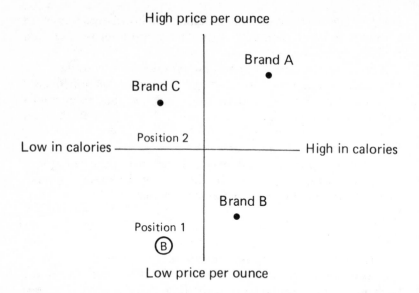

Figure 8. *Brand-positioning map*

Test marketing

When the product has been developed in line with your commercial expectations and the limitations of the market place, you are ready to test market more widely. Basically, there are four considerations to be taken into account.

- When to launch the product: If the product is replacing an existing one, should the stocks of the old product be run down? If demand is seasonal and the season is well advanced, should the launch be postponed until next season?
- Where to launch the product: It is important to choose an area where rapid acceptance and payback can be achieved rather than launching it in the stronghold of a competitor.
- To whom to launch the product: Often, certain sections of the population are more open to new ideas than others and so are willing to try it. These should be the first segment targeted.
- How should you launch your product? A clear promotion strategy needs to be planned to get PR, advertising and selling to reinforce each other and produce optimum results.

Checklist

- Examine your present offering on the three levels indicated.

Which additions to your existing offer at any of the three levels should enhance the value of your offering in your customers' eyes? Which deletions would enable you to save costs without decreasing the value of your offering?

- Examine the product mix. Is there sufficient opportunity for growth with a narrow mix for you to enjoy some of the benefits of concentration? Can you capitalise on a well-established reputation in the market place to increase the width of your mix? Which lines, by increasing their depth, would widen the spectrum of customers you can attract? Have your customers a clear image of your firm and your business objective or should you increase the consistency of your product mix?

- Do you manage your product mix? Does your mix include the growth products or services? Can you increase your sales and profitability by bringing underused resources into your business? Prepare a profitability analysis: How dependent is your business on low profitability business? Which high profit lines do you have that, given the right backing, could lift the overall profitability of your business? If you can persuade heavy users of the old product to adopt the new one, sales will climb rapidly. Where prospective customers are geographically close, sales costs will be minimised.

6
Pricing Decision

Pricing – the intractable problem

There are perhaps few decisions new entrepreneurs have to take where they feel more unsure of themselves than when they are trying to set the price for their new product or service. For many, what they fear most is that they will set the price too high and inhibit sales. Without a logical approach to pricing, many simply delegate the job to their accountant. Others simply set their price slightly below what they think is the 'going rate' or market price.

This is a strange and negligent way of using a major marketing tool, particularly, when as is so often the case, considerable care has been devoted to the design of the product and to studying the market. In the authors' experience, this preoccupation with avoiding a price that is too high often results in a price that is too low, and this can be equally damaging.

If your sales take the form of infrequent large orders, such as contracts, one seriously underpriced project may be enough to bankrupt you.

If you discover later on that you have set your price too low, it is often very difficult to adjust it upwards once your product or service and its price have become known. Dropping a price or not increasing it in line with inflation is much easier.

Customers are often very suspicious of new products and even more distrustful of new services offered at a price lower than those of existing products, since they suspect that the lower prices have been achieved by cutting corners on the quality. The price you affix to your product or service is, in many ways, a signal to the market of the value you place on your product.

When pricing is handled sensitively, on the other hand, it can have a dramatic effect on the profitability of the firm.

All the other elements of the marketing mix that can increase profits, such as a better quality product or packaging, better distribution or more advertising or sales staff, all involve the firm in higher costs and investments, which you hope will pay off. If you are able to command even a marginally higher price on the other hand, you can often increase your profits with far less risk. When your margins are slim, this effect can be particularly striking, as Example 18 illustrates.

Example 18. Finding the right pricing policy

A toothpaste manufacturer is contemplating launching a product to sell at around £1 per tube. The margins and profits he anticipates for this pricing policy are set out on in the table below. After studying the market carefully, he thinks he may just be able to achieve an extra 5p per tube without losing sales. As can be seen from the table, the effect on profitability for such a small difference in price can be dramatic!

Price per unit	Sales volume	Profit per unit	Total profits	Increase in price	Increase in profit- ability
£1.00	1000	20p	£200	–	–
£1.05	1000	25p	£250	5%	25%

Looked at another way, if the manufacturer was too nervous to pursue the higher pricing policy, he would have to sell 25 per cent more to achieve the same level of profitability.

Achieving a marginally better price is often easier than achieving a dramatic increase in sales

Towards a pricing strategy

There is no infallible means of setting the right price. Different firms at different times have to use pricing to achieve quite different market objectives. Price cutting and the sacrifice of profitability may be the best course for one firm to re-establish its market position in the short term. For another, because of its financial position, this option may be disastrous.

Whatever your objective, pricing is as much an art as a science. What is proposed in the following sequence by which all the relevant factors that impinge upon price can be considered in a logical manner. These factors are:

● cost considerations
● demand considerations

- competition considerations
- marketing considerations.

Cost considerations

All prices must, in the long term, cover the costs of generating and marketing the product or service and produce a reasonable profit. One approach is, therefore, to establish the costs, add a 'reasonable' profit margin and thus arrive at a price. This 'cost plus mark-up' approach has two major weaknesses, however:

- The difficulties of establishing what the true costs are.
- The possibility of your resulting price being *below* what the market is willing to pay.

It is inappropriate to attempt to cover all aspects of costing here. These are best left to a standard accountancy text. Marketers, however, do need to have a grasp of how costing works and, in particular, what its limitations are for establishing the market price.

The standard cost approach

To manage any business you need to know not just what your total costs are but the costs for each unit of product or service you are selling, the so-called 'standard cost'. You can then monitor your costs over the year to see that they are not running out of control.

To arrive at this cost, you need to establish:

- what sales you anticipate for that product;
- which costs are directly attributable to that product.

Example 19 shows a simplified example of how such costs are arrived at for a product such as cardboard boxes. First, the cost of labour and raw materials involved in making them can be fairly easily identified. Added together, these form the 'direct costs' for that product. There are other costs, however, which are more general in nature, including the heating, lighting, marketing, administration and management of the whole firm. These are shown as 'overheads'. If there are several products, these overheads will have to be shared between them and included in their cost calculations. In the example the overheads amount to £10.

To establish your prices you therefore need to establish at the beginning of each year what your costs will be. You do this by forecasting your sales; that is, the number of units you expect to sell in the coming year ('sales volume forecasting'). You then calculate the total costs involved in making and selling that quantity ('total costs'). By dividing the number of units you expect to sell into your total costs you thus arrive at the cost per unit ('unit costs'). If you now identify what profit you need to make overall, as a fair return for your efforts, you can work out the profit you need to make on each unit by dividing the profit figure by the number of units we expect to sell. This is normally expressed as a profit margin, as shown.

Example 19. Standard costing and pricing of cardboard boxes

	1988	1989
Sales volume forecast	20 units	30 units
Direct costs:		
Materials	£7	£10.50
Labour	£3	£4.50
Overheads	£10	£10
Total costs	£20	£25
Unit costs	$\frac{£20}{20} = £1$	$\frac{£20}{30} = £0.83$
Total profit required	£10	£15
Profit to be added to unit cost	$\frac{£10}{20} = £0.50$	$\frac{£15}{30} = £0.50$
Standard selling price	£1.50	£1.33
Mark-up on total cost	50%	50%

One of the problems of the standard cost approach is floating costs. Example 19 also shows what happens when the process is repeated a year later. Because of increased demand, the forecast has now gone up to 30 units.

In this example, as so often happens in real life, the extra production has been achieved without any extra management or extra buildings being necessary. The total cost of overheads has thus not been increased. The standard costs have thus decreased and since the cost plus mark-up system has been applied mechanically, so has the price.

If the increased demand has come about from the success of the product, there is absolutely no need to decrease prices. Indeed, if you are struggling to keep up with demand, this may result in exacerbating the situation by creating demand you cannot meet. It will be clear, therefore, that the cost plus mark-up method, although it has its uses in setting the lowest level of price below which you should not go, is extremely insensitive for arriving at the optimum price. You need to treat the price separately from the costs if you are not to become a victim of the system you have chosen.

There is another type of difficulty in applying the cost plus mark-up approach, which is how to cost unexpected additional business which you had not included in your forecast. If your manufacturer at some time in 1988, after having calculated his standard costs, was then asked to quote for an unexpected additional or 'marginal business' order for an overseas buyer for, say, 10 units, how should he calculate the costs involved and arrive at an appropriate price?

The formula should be:

Price for 10 units = standard cost per unit × no of units
$$= £1 × 10$$
$$= £10$$

If you again examine how the costs are made up in Example 19 it becomes clear that this standard cost will include 10 × £0.5 = £5 for overheads. If fulfilling this order again involves no increase in overheads, a total of £10 + £5 = £15 has been allocated for overheads, which is £5 more than is needed. The manufacturer could well be overcosting and overpricing on this order and stands a good chance of losing this opportunity of extra profit to a competitor who is using a more subtle costing approach.

Example 20. The problems of allocating overheads

	Product A			Product B		
Sales volume forecast	20 units			40 units		
Price per unit	£1			£1		
Sales revenue forecast	£20			£40		
Direct costs:						
Materials	£7			£5		
Labour	£3			£15		
Total direct costs	£10			£20		
Methods of allocating						
£15 overheads	(½)	(⅓)	(⅙)	(½)	(⅔)	(⅚)
Overheads share	£7.50	£5	£2.50	£7.50	£10	£12.50
Total costs	£17.50	£15	£12.50	£27.50	£30	£32.50
Profits	£2.50	£5	£7.50	£12.50	£10	£7.50
Profit margin	12.5%	2.5%	38%	30%	25%	19%

Example 20 shows a manufacturer using the same costing methods, but he is now manufacturing two products, product A and product B, as shown. The direct costs for each product are once again worked out. The total overheads for his factory and marketing are in this case £15. The problem he now faces is to allocate these overheads between the two products.

The first method used is very straightforward. Since there are two products, the overheads are divided equally between the two product lines. On that basis, as will be seen, product B has a much higher profit margin than A. He would therefore be well advised to try to sell more of product B instead of A, since by selling more of his profitable line he will increase his overall profit.

Most accountants would, however, object to this approach. Since the sales of product B are twice that of A, the former are likely to take up more space in the warehouse and more management attention. A fairer split would be to allocate the overheads as shown in the second method. Since the sales of product A are one-third of the total sales, it should only be allocated one-third of the overheads. Similarly, product B is now allocated two-thirds of the overhead burden.

This approach results in quite a different profit margin for one product relative to the other. As can be seen, each product is equally profitable, and pushing one product instead of the other, which the first method suggested, would not affect profitability.

The third method follows an approach that some accountants would argue is even fairer, since each product has a different labour content. Product B uses five times the amount of labour that A uses. It can therefore be argued that it takes five times the amount of supervision, space and wear and tear on the premises. A fairer division of the overheads is, therefore, one-sixth of overheads to be allocated to A and five-sixths to B. The effect on the profitability of B is quite startling. Had the manufacturer followed the strategy suggested by the first method and pushed product B, he could *decrease* his overall profitability by substituting sales of product B for those of product A.

The question as to which approach is correct is, on the other hand, difficult to answer. A good accountant tries to select the method he thinks is fairest. A marketer, however, needs a different approach to costing to help him make his decisions on profits and prices.

An improved costing approach – variable costing and the concept of contribution
A method of costing that helps to overcome some of the problems for the marketer is that of variable costing. Under this system,

costs are reallocated into categories other than direct costs and overheads. Because of the way that costs vary with the volume of sales, the costs are first recategorised into those that vary with sales volume and those that, within reason, do not.

Those costs that change with different volumes are designated 'variable' costs. Those that do not change with differing sales volume are designated 'fixed' costs. This approach helps to solve some of the problems of standard costing, as illustrated by the following:

Marginal business. Recalculating the figures in Example 19 in terms of fixed and variable costs, the costing is as follows:

Variable costs = £10
Fixed costs = £10
Total costs for 20 units = £20
Variable cost per unit = £0.50

If the manufacturer now wishes to quote for the marginal business, he proceeds as follows. Since fixed costs are already covered by his normal business of 20 units, the only costs to be covered by the marginal business are the variable costs themselves:

Variable costs for 10 units = £0.50 × 10 = £5

He now knows, without having to recalculate all his costs, that if he charges more than the variable costs of £0.50 each, he will make a profit.

Variable costing of this kind can thus be extremely useful, particularly where overheads are covered by orders at normal mark-up and separate opportunities exist to fill machine or production capacity. A producer can afford to price this business on a lower basis than he otherwise would and make profits which he would otherwise miss.

This approach must be used with care, however:

- If you do not obtain enough business at full mark-up to cover your fixed costs, your overall profits will tumble. This can certainly happen if you start accepting orders at the lower price from customers who should normally pay the full price.
- If the extra business exceeds capacity, extra premises or machinery are then required, and marginal business will have to bear these extra fixed costs.

The allocation of overheads. Variable costing can also help to solve some of the problems of the allocation of overheads, as illustrated in Example 20. This entails the calculation of each product's 'contribution', which is defined as:

Contribution of product A = sales revenue of product A −
variable costs of product A

Each product can be envisaged, therefore, as contributing to covering all fixed costs and necessary profits, as shown in Figure 9. The sum of the contributions thus covers the fixed costs and produces the profits needed in the business.

This method also provides a more convenient yardstick to help assess the profitability of each product – the contribution each makes to fixed costs and overheads.

Thus, in judging the relative profitability of the two products, as in Example 20, the calculations are as follows:

$$
\begin{aligned}
\text{Contribution of product A} &= \text{£20} - \text{£10} \\
&= \text{£10} \\
\text{Contribution per unit} &= \frac{\text{£10}}{\text{£20}} = \text{£0.50}
\end{aligned}
$$

$$
\begin{aligned}
\text{Contribution of product B} &= \text{£40} - \text{£20} \\
&= \text{£20} \\
\text{Contribution per unit} &= \frac{\text{£20}}{\text{£40}} = \text{£0.50}
\end{aligned}
$$

In this example, the contribution per unit of each product is therefore identical. Selling more of one product rather than the other will not increase the profitability. However, this method has made it possible to arrive at the correct decision with far less complications than judging between products simply on the basis of profitability margins alone.

Judging between projects when production capacity is limited. The contribution method has a further useful application when setting priorities between different products or orders. Many small firms have limited production capacity. At times of peak demand, when they may not be able to take on all the work they could get, they have to be sure that the work they choose to perform will yield the maximum return. By using the contribution method, this can be decided fairly rapidly.

Example 21 shows how it is done. Although the size of both jobs is the same, job A yields a higher contribution. If there is more work available than the printer's machinery can handle, he has to calculate what contribution each job will yield per machine hour, since this is the factor in short supply. On this basis, job B gives the printer a better yield per hour and also gives him two extra machine hours that he can use on another job. Job B should thus be chosen.

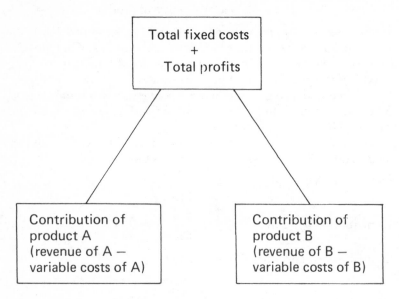

Figure 9. *The concept of contribution*

Example 21.   How a jobbing printer uses the concept of contribution to choose between two jobs, when production capacity is limited

A jobbing printer has filled most of his production capacity for the month. However, he has a limited amount of production capacity left and has to choose between two orders. The question is, which job should he choose?

	Job A	Job B
Price per unit	£1	£1
No of units	300	300
Price for job	£300	£300
Variable costs of job	£225	£240
Contribution of job	£75	£60
Machine hours for job	7.5	5
Contribution per machine hour for each job	£10	£12

Establishing the costs of professional services. Many self-employed people such as researchers, translators, counsellors or consultants find it difficult to establish the hourly or daily cost of their time when, as they say, they are not paying an employee. So in real terms their own time costs them nothing. Although there may be professional associations such as the Institute of Linguists who can provide guidelines as to what price their members should charge, without guidelines as to their costs, they do not know what margin they have to play with in a competitive situation.

Often such professionals find the contribution concept helpful, the contribution they have to achieve being the salary and overheads costs they need to cover over the year. Their calculations might run as outlined in Example 22.

Example 22. How a professional uses the concept of contribution to assess costs

The overall contribution the business should make equals personal salary plus overheads (eg pension, insurance, car, telephone, equipment), as follows:

$$£20,000 + £5,000 = £25,000$$

The number of working hours available to the business in a year are:

52 weeks × 40 hours = 2,080 hours

less 2 weeks holiday (2 × 40 hours):

(80 hours) = 2,000 hours

less 1 week provision for sickness (1 = 40 hours):

(40 hours) = 1,960 hours

less 1 day per week for marketing and administration (49 × 8 hours):

(392 hours) = 1,568 hours

less provision for hours remaining unsold to clients:

(68 hours) = 1,500 hours

Cost of each hour is:

$$\frac{\text{Contribution required from the business}}{\text{Productive hours available for sale}} = \frac{£25,000}{1,500 \text{ hours}}$$

$$= £16 \text{ per hour}$$

Demand considerations

In setting your price, you also need to take account of the effect your price will have on your sales volumes. Figure 10(a) illustrates how differences in prices can affect the demand for a given product. A manufacturer wanted to see what the effects of different prices could be so he tried selling his product at different prices and measured the effect on the amount he sold. At a price of £10, 10,000 units were sold. When the price was cut to £5, 15,000 units were sold in a similar period. By repeating these experiments for different prices he was able, by plotting them on a graph, to produce a curve or 'demand schedule' joining these results. He could thus read off all combinations of volume and price between these two fixed price levels. For example, if he were to set the price at £7.50 the demand should be about 10,000 units.

The manufacturer can now calculate the effect on the sales revenue of setting the price for this product at different levels.

Price	Units sold	Revenue
£10	5,000	£50,000
£7.50	10,000	£75,000
£5	15,000	£75,000

Although dropping the price from £10 to £7.50 has increased revenue substantially, the decrease from £7.50 to £5 has not increased the revenue at all! More units have been sold and he has worked harder, but he has not increased revenue. At the same time, the effects on his profits have probably been catastrophic! Before setting your price low, in order to maximise sales, therefore, be very careful to establish the effect the price drop will have on your sales revenue.

For most products, the sensitivity of revenue to price is far less than you might believe. Where there is little difference between brands, price sensitivity is, of course, likely to be high, and small price differences may result in appreciable increases in demand. Most branded products, as opposed to commodity items, are specifically designed, however, to be different from what the competition is offering. All promotional efforts are geared towards making the product stand out from its competitors.

Price is not, therefore, always the first or only consideration: quality workmanship and design may well be more important to the buyer. The price differences are also not normally as great as those shown in Figure 10(a). For most branded goods and marketed services, the demand schedule resembles Figure 10(b)

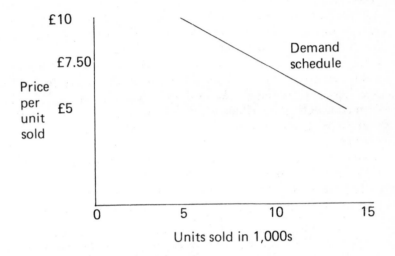

Figure 10(a). *Example of a price-sensitive product demand schedule*

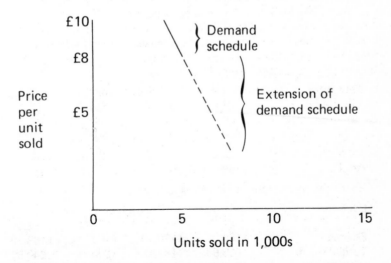

Figure 10(b). *Example of the demand schedule of a branded product. Only two experimental prices were used: £8 and £10. The dotted part of the graph is the logical extension of the demand schedule to cover other prices*

much more closely. The steepness of the slope illustrates the fact that decreases in price will result in no increase or an actual decrease in revenue.

One of the most important issues you need to establish, therefore, before launching a new product is whether your demand schedule is flattened, rather like Figure 10(a), or steep, such as in Figure 10(b). If your market research indicates that it is more likely to be steep, you will maximise your revenue and profits by pitching the price higher rather than lower.

In considering the effect of the demand schedule when setting your price, it is important to realise that a price which maximises sales revenue may not necessarily produce the optimum profitability in terms of contribution. To estimate optimum profitability, you need to take into consideration the variable costs involved, as well as the sales revenue, as illustrated in Example 23.

Example 23. Setting the price

A manufacturer is trying to establish the optimum price for a wood-cutting machine he is developing. The price should, he thinks, be somewhere in the region of £1,000 to £2,000. He asks his three distributors, A, B and C, to give him a forecast of how much they could sell in their territory at each of four different price points, £1,000, £1,200, £1,600 and £2,000, so that he can calculate a demand schedule.

He has calculated the variable costs per unit at £600 per machine.

He has invested £100,000 in development and launching costs and would like to know when the product will yield enough contribution to cover this investment.

The sales forecast in units is as follows:

Distributor	Price per unit			
	£1.0	£1.20	£1.60	£2.0
A	70	60	40	24
B	80	62	50	36
C	6	20	10	8
Total	156	142	100	68

He then processes these figures as follows:

Costings	Price per unit			
	£1.0	£1.20	£1.60	£2.0
Revenue	£156	£170.40	£160	£163.20
Variable costs	£93.60	£85.20	£60	£40.80
Contribution	£62.40	£85.20	£100	£122.40
Payback period in years	1.6	1.2	1.0	0.8

The decision as to which price he wishes to select depends very much upon his company objectives:

- If he wishes to maximise his revenue, he will choose a price of £1,200.
- If he wishes to maximise the number of units sold, he will choose a price of £1000.
- If he wishes to achieve the maximum profitability and recover his fixed investments as quickly as possible, he will choose the top price of £2,000.

Further uses of the demand concept

Entrepreneurs who believe that the demand for their service or product is not over-sensitive to price, use price to control demand. For example, plumbers or building contractors who are working close to their capacity because of heavy demand are loathe to refuse or turn away an enquiry from a potential customer, so as not to discourage them from coming back to them on some future occasion. A common approach they use is to quote either a longer delivery or an inflated price.

If the contractor does not get the job, he is not too worried at this stage. On the other hand, if he does get the job at this price, it might well compensate for the bother of rescheduling existing contracts or even paying overtime rates to his staff.

Whenever you are working at capacity and demand is exceeding your capacity, increased prices can throttle back demand to a level where you can cope, while ensuring that the business you are taking is the most profitable.

Example 24. Managing demand by pricing

Ted was a qualified pipe fitter and for the last five years had worked as a maintenance foreman for a public utility. Having been given the opportunity to retire early on an enhanced pension, he decided to accept the offer and set up his own plumbing business, where he could do a good job for a reasonable price.

Since he would be receiving his pension, his need for money was modest. Also, he would be working from home, so his costs would be modest. He was therefore happy to charge out his work at £5 per hour.

Ted was quite surprised to find that the demand for his service was soon exceeding the hours he intended to work and he found it impossible to meet all requests. He considered taking on new staff, but could not cover the salaries with the amount he was charging. At long last, Ted discovered the penalty for underpricing. It emerged that all the subcontracting work he was doing was for a local building contractor, who was charging out the work to the client at £15 per hour, whereas Ted was only getting £5.

Ted put up his prices to bring them closer to the prevailing charges plumbers were making. Demand settled back to the point where the customers he was getting chose him for his good workmanship and his dependability. Ted now has the kind of business he wants, rather than being chased to death by those who only wished to exploit someone they knew was undercharging.

Competition considerations

The prices charged by competitors must also be taken into account in your pricing policies. Certainly, they give you a benchmark against which to position your own price. It is poor policy, however, simply to undercut a competitor's price, particularly if your product possesses appreciable advantages over that of your competitors. Most customers expect to pay more for better products or services.

Quantifying benefits

Sometimes it is possible to quantify the value of the different features your product brings to your customer. Products or services sold to offices or factories can be evaluated in terms of time saved, extra profits earned, space saved and lower maintenance costs compared with competitive products, as shown in Example 25. In the example 'your' product, in this case a machine used in a manufacturing process, is more efficient. However, the competitive machine takes up slightly less room on the factory floor.

Example 25. Quantifying the benefits of your product against a competitor's product

Benefits per annum	Your machine	Competitor's machine
Savings on spoilt product	£20	–
Saving on fuel consumption	£80	–
Value of extra output	£600	–
Savings on maintenance costs	£100	–
Value of space saved in factory:		
rent	–	£20
rates	–	£10
Total	£800	£30

If the competitor's price is £6,000, the difference in benefits you are offering amount to £800 − £30 = £770 per year of operation. If you were to propose a price of £7,155, the difference of £1,155 would be paid for in 18 months; thereafter the product would produce annual savings of £770 compared with the competitive machine. This difference in price is, therefore, easy to justify.

Rating benefits
At times it is not so easy to reduce the differences to one common denominator. Different features of the product may have different importance for your customers. Table 4 (overleaf) illustrates how you can get customers to:

- list the product features they consider important;
- indicate the 'relative importance' of each feature by dividing the 'weighting coefficients' (out of a total of 100 shared between these features);
- rate the performance of each product for each of these factors out of a possible 10 marks ('rating'). Finally, an 'overall rating score' can be obtained by multiplying the coefficient by the individual rating, and summing this figure for each product. The difference in the final score should be reflected in the price differential. In this case, based on these ratings $((824 − 731)/731 \times 100)$ you would be justified in charging up to 12.5 per cent more than your competitor.

In both the foregoing cases, the final differences in price must be decided with sensitivity. Where the differences these procedures produce are large, you have to test whether the price difference is perceived by your target customers as rational. Similarly, if you are too timid, and set the gap too close, you need to test whether the consumer begins to disbelieve that the claims you are making for better quality are true. Strangely enough, customers will often not even believe a product is of a higher quality unless there is a higher price tag to draw the consumers' attention to the quality.*

---

* Certainly this is the experience of American researchers examing housewives' blind testing of carpets of different qualities offered at random prices. Where high quality carpet was offered at low prices, it was rated lower than inferior qualities at their normal price. See Wheatly, Chiu and Goldman, *Journal of Retailing*, Vol 57, No 2, 1981.

Product features	Weighting coefficient	Your product		Competitor's product	
		Individual rating	Overall rating	Individual rating	Overall rating
Ruck facility	14	8	112	9	126
Hem facility	16	7	112	8	128
Buttonhole facility	14	9	126	7	98
Embroidery movement	20	8	160	6	120
Reverse movement	20	8	160	6	120
Operation by hand	11	9	99	9	99
Portability/weight	10	8	80	7	70
Total	100		824		731

Table 4. *Rating of two competitive sewing machines to establish which price should be relative to the competitor*

Services
Services need special attention when you are positioning prices against competitors. Consumers who have never used a particular service before are very dependent upon any clues to help them judge the relative quality of the service offered by one supplier compared to another. Any one clue assumes great importance therefore. If the service concerns their vital interests, such as their health or prosperity, the main criterion governing their choice is whether you understand and can meet their needs better than the competition. Your main task is, therefore, to convince them that you are offering a quality, dependable service.

A substantially lower price offered by one supplier thus makes consumers very suspicious that that supplier has not understood their needs, and this suspicion will persist even if they place an order.

The wisest policy when marketing services is, therefore, to ensure that your prices are at least comparable with your competitors. Where better quality or dependability can be demonstrated, a higher price should be quoted and justified. There are few brain surgeons who succeed by offering cut-price operations!

Marketing considerations
There are four major considerations, each of which will be discussed in turn.

Price plateaux
For many products there is a 'going price' which it can be dangerous to go below. Most drinks served in bars, such as wine served by the glass, are priced not simply on the basis of cost. Instead, they are priced in line with other drinks served there, such as pints of beer. Several manufacturers of alternatives to beer and spirits, such as fruit juices, have found that having priced their drinks too low, the drinks are considered too cheap to qualify as an adult drink. An uplift of prices to the plateau of a bar drink, as well as a repackaging to justify the price change, has increased sales tremendously.

The image of high price
If you wish to use up-market distributors to distribute your goods, the image which your goods project reflects on them. Thus, low-priced goods are often not taken on by such distributors because

they damage the image of the store. Similarly, if the target market is a group to whom status is important, a higher price than less respected brands increases acceptability, even though the costs are not that different from low-priced alternatives. The examples of accessories by such manufacturers as Yves Saint Laurent are cases in point, where the brand name prominently displayed on the article often justifies a higher price than a similar accessory produced by other less well-respected manufacturers. The higher price makes the product more exclusive.

Price barriers

Price barriers also exist for many goods. When they do occur, customers can be persuaded that what they have paid is reasonable, so long as the price does not exceed a certain limit. Do not be misled by the thought that *you* would not take this view (if you are honest, you might well do!). This applies no matter how close the price approaches the top unit of that bracket. Prices such as £3.95 seem to focus on £3.00 as the price, rather than £4.00. If other considerations suggest £3.60 as a reasonable price, £3.95 may give an extra margin of profit without decreasing sales. This also produces an automatic security measure, in some businesses, as staff must 'ring up' the sale to give change.

Price ranges

Price ranges are also possible for different market segments. Often, there are real opportunities for higher profits, if you can identify different market segments where price sensitivity is appreciably different. One professional bookkeeper, for example, charged a fixed fee to all her clientele for putting their ledgers and accounts in order. She soon found that shopkeepers, being more methodical, were causing her far less work, whereas building contractors lost invoices and bills, causing her endless trouble. Contractors themselves considered keeping books a nuisance and a mystery and laid great store by her help. She now charges quite different rates according to the profession of her clients. Her profits have improved and both sets of clients are happy to pay what she is asking.

Putting the policy together

Having explored all four dimensions of the pricing question, you need to decide which level of price you will set. There remain four basic issues to be resolved.

Why did you introduce this product?

A new product can come about in two different ways: either to fill spare capacity or, since it represents a departure for the firm, it may require new plant or new investment. As noted earlier, if you have already covered your overheads and are using spare capacity, you can use marginal costing and lower prices. If it is a long-term commitment to the market involving long-term, exclusive use of the equipment, you will have to use full mark-up and pricing.

Should you adopt a policy of skimming the cream?

It is not uncommon to launch a new product that is demonstrably superior to other products available at a higher price than its rivals. This is done consciously in the knowledge that the volume sold will be small, but the profit margins or 'cream' will be high.

The advantages of such a policy are:

- For a new product, because of its novelty, price is often of secondary importance. Later, when competition emerges, price may become more important. At this point, the price can be lowered.
- High profit margins mean that cash is available to you to ensure good advertising and a well-funded launch.
- Initial investments can be recovered quickly and risk is thus reduced.
- You have the flexibility to feel out the nature of the demand, by testing whether the quality message can offset the higher price.
- If you have limited production capacity, excessive demand and delays in delivery could initially cause loss of customer goodwill. A limited demand avoids these problems.
- It is always easier to ease the price downwards as the product becomes established.

The disadvantages are:

- High profits will tempt competitors to launch their own versions of the product.
- Low volumes may disrupt factory schedules.
- If the price is off-putting, the product may take some time to take off and gain acceptance.
- If an economic depression occurs at the time of the launch, customers may have to sacrifice the benefits of the new product in order to remain within reduced budgets.

Should you attempt a penetration price policy?

An alternative policy is to attempt to get quick acceptance by low prices at the launch so as to achieve high volumes quickly.

The advantages of such a policy are:

- Moving quickly into high volume production may bring about lower costs.
- If the margins are slim, competitors will not be so eager to launch their own product.
- If the product is accepted quickly, you can gain a wide allegiance for the future.
- Demand for the product is less vulnerable to economic downturns.

The disadvantages are:

- Since margins are low, the profits are a long time arriving, This increases the risk that if adverse conditions develop in the meantime, the delay might be even longer and the product never becomes profitable.
- The financial build-up is slow. Plant and investment have to be amortised over a long period.
- If price is really set too low initially, there may be real problems in adjusting it to a higher level later, without revamping the product substantially.

What will the competitors do?

Your policy cannot be decided in a vacuum. The countermeasures that the competitors are likely to take must be assessed before a final decision is taken, as follows:

- How vulnerable are they to a lower price product being launched? If your product threatens to take away the major part of their business, they will be forced to defend themselves.
- If you introduce a high price policy, the reaction may well be to move their own prices up; if they have been depressed in the past, there will be no counter-attack.
- An alternative strategy is to further cut their prices and upset the balance you had created between benefits and prices, making your product very vulnerable indeed.

Pricing tactics – cut-price and discounting existing products

This is quite a different use of pricing as a marketing weapon and is normally used to stimulate the sales of existing products or services.

There are several problems associated with its use, as follows:

- It is a tactical weapon. It can be used to improve your market position temporarily. You cannot use this weapon as a long-term measure, since your competitors are bound to react and restore the status quo – possibly reducing the profitability for all.
- Once a going price is established, consumers start looking for bargains by 'magpie shopping'. A full-scale price war can ensue to everyone's disadvantage.

Price cutting can be effective, however, where:

- demand is elastic, since it can increase sales volume;
- margins are high.

Checklist

- If you have already started trading, how did you arrive at your pricing strategy?
- Which costing system does your accountant use? If he uses standard costing, how does he allocate overheads? Could he provide a system that will enable you to use contribution to calculate the relative profiability of your product lines and choose between different opportunities?
- Have you used different price levels to determine the price sensitivity of demand for your product? If not, how will you set about it?
- Can you use the demand schedule method to control demand at a time of overloading or spare capacity?
- Does the difference in price between your product and that of your competitor reflect the relative merits of each?
- Is there a price plateau you must respect and can you move your price up nearer to a price barrier?
- Can you identify a sector where your service or product incurs more costs or is more valued by the client? Can you run two price levels and add more profits to your firm?
- Given your company circumstances, which policy is best, a 'skimming the cream' policy or a 'market penetration' policy?

7
Distribution

What is distribution?

'Distribution is the means by which the output of a producer is made available to the target consumer.'

Most articles customers use are manufactured or produced many miles from where they buy them. Nevertheless, customers expect to find them:

- available when and where they need them;
- in quantities that suit them;
- in surroundings that enable them to make a good choice between products;
- with access to other services to help them use the product, such as after-sales service.

The purpose of distribution is, therefore, to provide all that is necessary to transform a product on a factory floor into an attractive purchase at the point of sale. Distribution is a key element in influencing your customers to buy and retaining their loyalty afterwards, so that they buy again.

If your product is not available when the customer wants it, or where he normally buys this type of product, he will substitute another, and all your other marketing efforts will have been in vain.

Distribution of services

Any service needs planned distribution to ensure that the target customer has access to it. For example:

- A hairdresser or tobacconist who is aiming at the passing trade

strives to get premises where pedestrian traffic is heaviest.
- Florists set up stands outside offices and factories on a Friday to tempt the workers who have just drawn their pay packets to celebrate the weekend with a bunch of flowers.

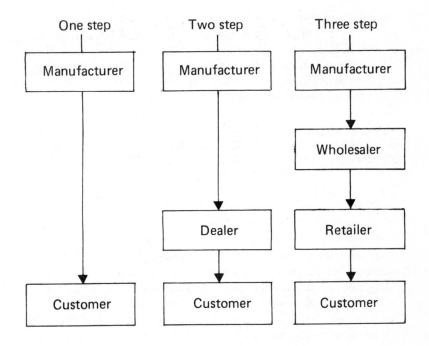

Figure 11. *Different forms of distributive channels*

Distributive channels

Distribution consists, therefore, of both the physical movement of goods to points close to the customer and also the provision of the right environment and staff at the point of sale to help complete the transaction. Both these elements make up the distributive channels. These channels can take several forms, as shown in Figure 11.

One-step channels
In this type of channel, the manufacturer deals directly with the customers. This is a fairly common form of distribution in the selling of computers, large building contracts or where manufac-

turers sell by direct mail.

The manufacturer in this case takes on all the responsibility for the selling, delivery, invoicing and servicing of his products, and deals direct with the final customer.

Two-step channels

For many products, it is possible to identify specialist selling or retailing organisations which are already in touch with the customers the manufacturer wishes to do business with. If these intermediaries can be persuaded to add your product to the assortment of goods they handle, they can perform the role of distributor for you. Thus supermarkets, DIY superstore and builders' merchants buy direct from the manufacturers and sell these goods on their behalf. Similarly, insurance agents act as a go-between for purchasers of insurance and the insurance firms.

Three-step channels

In this case, the job of the intermediary has been split into two levels. Small independent grocers and hardware retailers sell the same sort of assortment of goods as their supermarket rivals. Since their sales of each item are so much smaller, however, they cannot afford either to buy or stock in the same quantities. They need a wholesaler to take over these functions and act as a go-between with the manufacturer. Wholesalers, by reminding the retailers of the manufacturer's product, also take over a part of the selling function from the manufacturer. If they did not exist, the manufacturer would have to perform this function himself.

Combined patterns

There are many occasions when manufacturers find it useful to combine single- and multi-stage channels for particular purposes, as follows:

Different products. Some manufacturers deal with their normal customers via dealers. However, they would process large government or overseas tenders direct, since they expect a big discount for quantity.

Different uses. Avon Rubber sell their tyres to Rolls-Royce for fitting to new cars. The manufacturers act as a kind of wholesaler and expect low prices. However, Avon sell replacement tyres through garages, since they can normally get higher prices when they use these channels.

Why use intermediaries?

In using distributors, you are delegating an essential element of your marketing mix to an outside organisation, and manufacturers only do this if there are good reasons for it. For instance:

- Distributive intermediaries provide you with a ready-made network of contacts that would take you years to establish at a cost you may not be able to afford.
- Distributors provide an environment that the customer needs in order to make a choice. If different competing brands need to be compared, this can be done by the customer in the supermarket. If a local firm or a well-known distributor stocks your product, it may enhance the credibility of your product in the eyes of a consumer.
- Distributors can spread the costs of stocking and selling your goods over all the brands they carry, thereby distributing your products at a lower cost than you can.
- Because of local knowledge or by selling on a cash basis, instead of your having to do it by direct mail, their cost of bad debts is lower than it would be for you.
- Since the distributor is rewarded by a discount off the selling price, you are not risking your capital in holding local stocks.
- Distributors have good specialist knowledge of retailing or distribution, which you may not possess.

On the other hand, distributors may cause these problems:

- They are not as committed to your product as you are. If the customer prefers another, they will substitute it.
- They may use the manufacturer's product as a loss leader.
- They may drop the product from their list if they believe they can make a better profit with another line.
- They expect the manufacturer to stimulate demand for the product; for example, by advertising or providing display material.

The question of whether to deal direct with the consumer is, therefore, dependent first upon the availability of suitable channels and their willingness to add your product to their assortment. Second, you have to balance the economies of the distributors' lower selling and servicing costs with the disadvantages of not being present at the point where your customers are making their decisions, and thus having less control over the selling process.

Deciding which distribution channel to use

In deciding which distribution channel to use there are, in fact, six factors to ponder, each of which will be discussed in turn.

Customer characteristics
Distributors are generally required when customers are widely dispersed, there is a large number of them and they buy frequently in small amounts.

Product characteristics
Direct distribution is required when bulky products, such as soft drinks, are involved. Bulky products need channel arrangements that minimise the shipping distance and the number of handlings. Similarly, non-standard equipment often necessitates specialist knowledge which distributors do not possess, since the distributor has no role to play. Manufacturers of this equipment tend to deal direct.

Where high unit value can cover higher unit selling costs, manufacturers can keep control over distribution by dealing direct. Finally, products requiring installation or maintenance are generally sold through a limited network, such as sole agents (see below).

Distributor characteristics
Distributors are more useful when their skills of low cost contact, service and storage are more important than their lack of commitment to one brand. Some manufacturers of hardware find this is true where their brands have little effect on their customer loyalty.

Competitive characteristics
The channels you choose may often be influenced by the channels your competitors use. For example, some manufacturers seek to place their product close to that of their competitors: Burger King try to obtain sites next to McDonald's. On the other hand, some manufacturers, such as Avon Cosmetics, choose not to compete for scarce positions in retail stores and have established profitable door-to-door direct selling operations instead.

Company characteristics

The size of a company often correlates with its market share. The bigger its market share, the easier it is to find distributors willing to handle the product. Paradoxically, the more powerful a manufacturer is, the less he needs to rely on distributors. For example, if a manufacturer has ample financial resources at his disposal, he may decide to cover all marketing functions himself and to delegate only a small proportion of the functions to the distributors. A manufacturer of small domestic appliances, for example, may decide to make his own arrangements for after-sales service, rather than leave it to his dealers.

Similarly, where the company's product mix is broad, it increases the probability of a customer buying at least one item. It makes it more cost-effective to deal direct.

Finally, a policy of fast delivery is not compatible with a large number of stages in the channel and there is a tendency to deal direct.

Environmental characteristics

Changes in the economic and legal environment can also bring about changes in distributive structures. For example, when the market is depressed, manufacturers want to move their goods to market in the most economic way. They thus cut out intermediaries or inessential services to compete on price and deal direct. Again, legal restrictions have been introduced in recent years to prevent channel characteristics which 'may tend to substantially lessen competition'.

Finally, there may be legal restrictions on who may handle the product. For example, ethical drugs, those available on prescription, may only be sold through chemists and chemists' wholesalers.

Choosing the channel

In most situations, it is possible to identify several different types of channel or distributors. A firm deciding to market car radios, for example, has the following alternatives:

- Original equipment market: It could seek a contract with one or more manufacturers to buy its radios for factory installation on their cars.
- Car dealer market: It could sell the radios to various car dealers

for replacement sales when they service cars.

- Retail automotive parts dealer market: It could sell its radios to the public through retail automotive parts dealers. It could reach these dealers through its own sales force or via wholesalers.
- Mail order market: It could arrange to have its radio advertised in mail order catalogues and the DIY press.

Each alternative would be explored to see which channel or combination of channels best met the firm's objectives and constraints. However, the best choice of channel must take into account whether the manufacturer can control the distribution channel he has created.

Example 26. New technology and changes in distributive channel

Until fairly recently, amateur photographers used the local chemist both to supply them with film and also to develop the exposed rolls. The chemist either developed them himself or acted as a dealing agent for a specialist film processor who served all the chemists in the neighbourhood.

This distribution system almost disappeared with the advent of the high speed, automatic, film developing machine. The machines processed and printed film so quickly that costs tumbled and infinitely larger throughputs were possible. If the owners of these machines could gain bigger markets, they could offer far lower prices than previously possible. They used national direct mail to persuade the general public to post the exposed film direct to the processors and processed tham at a fraction of the charge the chemists were demanding. The chemist shops were thus cut out completely.

Now the pendulum is swinging back again. Local processors have bought the same high speed equipment so their costs are now in line with the nationals. Being local, they can process and return the films within 48 hours or less, which is far faster than the postal service. They have now persuaded chemists to act as distributors once again, offering each a point-of-sale board and fixed competitive prices. All the chemists have to do is accept the films and place them in the envelope provided ready for collection, with little trouble to themselves. Chemists are now back competing in the film processing business.

The problems of managing the channel

Distributors are not passive parts of a channel but have their own ideas on what their role shall be. Unless this is resolved, the result will be unproductive friction.

Distributors, agents and stockists
In most channels, a manufacturer expects the 'distributors' to buy the goods for resale and take on the risks and costs of:

- storage and delivery
- shrinkage (ie loss from damage or theft);
- bad debts.

As the distributor is using his own capital, he is highly motivated to move the stock, and so plays an active part in selling the goods. Although the 'stockist' also buys the goods on his own account in response to requests from his customers, he expects the manufacturer to ensure high demand and, when this does not materialise, expects to be able to return the goods.

An 'agent', however, only takes the goods on consignment. Although the goods may be on his premises, they remain the property of the manufacturer and the risks remain with the manufacturer. Since his capital is not at risk, the agent is happy to sell to customers who may not pay, and instead of acting for the manufacturer, he refers all customer complaints back.

Thus, unless a clear, mutual understanding is reached as regards each partner's duties when setting up the distributive agreement, there will inevitably be problems and conflict.

Protecting the distributor's rights
Distributors need to understand what the manufacturer's intentions are. These are normally incorporated into the definition of the distributorship, which can take one of three forms:

Sole agency. This agreement is common when a distributor is required to make a substantial commitment or investment to provide services solely for one product or brand. To protect both parties, the distributor agrees not to stock competitive items and the manufacturer agrees not to appoint another distributor within the local area.

Exclusive distribution. This is common when a manufacturer wishes to protect the image of his product by channelling it through a limited number of outlets, even though these distributors are stocking competitive brands. For example, a manufacturer of expensive watches undertakes in his agreement with the jewellers who will retail his watches not to sell through department stores and only to appoint a limited number of jewellers as distributors.

Extensive distribution. Certain grocery products benefit from being placed alongside their competitors wherever they are displayed. Manufacturers of such products want their goods available in each grocer's store in the country.

Other products such as cigarettes and chewing gum need to be available to their consumers in every place by every possible means, such as corner shops, supermarkets, bars, hotels, trains, automatic dispensers, etc. Both manufacturer and distributor understand the need for such a policy and the benefit to both parties.

In general terms, therefore, unless the distribution policy clarifies the manufacturer's intentions, friction will result.

The growth of distributor power
In many channels, the greater volume of sales flows through a small number of large distributors. In the grocery business, for example, the top five supermarket chains sell nearly two-thirds of all groceries in the UK. If the manufacturer does not use these powerful distributors, he will not get access to a large part of his market. The distributor can exploit his position therefore:

- to squeeze preferential discounts from manufacturers. These are sometimes then used to cut the price of the product
- to force manufacturers to produce similar products to his own for the distributor. The distributor then sells these 'own brands' at a lower price.
- to limit the manufacturers' role to that of producing goods to the distributor's specification at the lowest possible mark-up.

Guidelines for channel leadership

Know your target market and keep in touch with it
- Few distributors will even consider taking on a new product unless they can be convinced that the market research has been done and the demand exists. They need to know which market segment the product is aimed at and whether it fits their customer franchise.

- Distributors would normally expect the manufacturer to be able to give them an idea of the sales they should be able to expect in their area.
- For most distributors, the best proof that potential exists is to show them orders that have already been taken for the product by direct mail.
- Even after the distributor has started selling the product, it is good practice to keep in touch with consumers who have bought it, to measure the success of your distribution. Problems can then be discussed jointly and remedial action taken as part of a partnership. No distributor likes to feel that, having taken in the stock from a manufacturer, he is then on his own.

Develop a clear distribution policy

When starting out, there is a great temptation to give the distributorship to anyone who will take it on. Take care; this may well lead to friction later on and distributors withdrawing. The principles that need to be defined are:

- Is it to be a sole agent, or an exclusive or extensive distribution policy?
- If sole agents or exclusive distributors are to be used, how will the territories be defined?
- If sole agents are appointed, will you credit them with sales that come to you direct?
- Under what conditions will you deal direct with customers?

What do you expect of the distributor?

- What size stock would you expect him to take in relation to his projected sales?
- What mix of products should he take?
- What selling effort do you expect of him?
- What display space will you expect?
- What do you expect him to do to promote the product?
- What customer franchises should he have?

What terms of trade will you work on?

- What terms of payment will you expect (30 days, discounts for early payments, etc)?
- What is your policy on returned items, or those which have been very slow to move?

- What delivery are you offering?
- What trade discount will you allow and what higher discounts for higher sales?

How will you motivate the distributor?

Manufacturers are often disappointed that simply demonstrating that their product is a good one does not guarantee a distributor will respond to the offer of a distributorship. You need to treat the distributor as a customer, understanding his needs and demonstrating how your agency will help him meet those needs. This takes time and demands regular and frequent contact. The considerations that will influence distributors are:

- Will your product help him to gain a lead over his competitors?
- Will your product help him to get the business of certain customers or types of customer he has not been able to attract?
- Will your product give him a better return than other products (margin × volume of sales)?
- Will your product fit in with the other products he sells?
- Will it enhance the sales of complementary products?
- Will your product give a high return for the small space it takes up in the stores or in the display area?
- Will you provide him with literature, point-of-sale material and help by training both his internal and external sales staff?
- Will you accompany him on visits to high potential users who he finds it difficult to sell to?

What resources will you devote to motivating your distributors?

- Who will be available to appoint distributors and maintain contact?
- What skills do you have for persuading a distributor to give prominence to your products?
- Can you teach the distributor's staff how to sell your product?
- Can you demonstrate how easy your product is to sell, by selling it in the showroom or in a customer's premises?
- Can you give distributor staff good selling arguments against competition?

Part 3
External Considerations

8

The Promotional Mix

Despite the emphasis on differentiation in previous chapters, few businesses are perceived as being unique. From your customers' point of view, you may appear to be one of a number of similar businesses; and for most, the world outside is increasingly competitive. Although there are some, who feel business will just arrive, like the apocryphal businessman who did not believe in advertising until he had to put a 'For Sale' notice outside his premises, most must accept that the world is unlikely to beat a path to their door unprompted. Some form of promotion is necessary. It is this that attracts business, preferably of specific sorts, in the required quantity and at the right time, and helps to distinguish you from the competition.

But like everything else in marketing it does not just happen. Successful promotional activity needs to be based on a continuous process of review, planning and implementation. And its inception demands time, skill and a systematic process.

Several different techniques are involved in what is called the communications, or promotional, mix. They include public and press relations (often abbreviated to PR), advertising (including direct mail) and sales promotion (including merchandising), all of which provide varying degrees of precision, creating a spectrum of awareness in relation to the customer, who is seen at the centre of the diagram in Figure 12. (Selling is reviewed in detail in Chapter 9.)

Whatever the technique, each is intended to play a part in the overall process of initiating, increasing and maintaining awareness of what you offer to your customers – your promotional plan. The intent is to move customers from total lack of awareness through to the point at which they actually buy. And, hopefully, buy again.

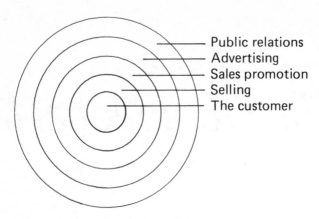

Figure 12. *The communications mix*

The buying process

The purpose of any promotion must be to change the attitudes of the target audience. Eventually, the aim is to change from non-usage of a product to usage or repeated usage. Diagrammatically, the stages in the buying process are as follows:

Unawareness

Awareness

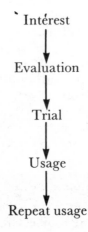

Interest

Evaluation

Trial

Usage

Repeat usage

Each stage represents a tangible change and is worth examining sequentially.

Unawareness → Awareness

This is the stage during which a buyer moves from no knowledge of a product or situation towards a position where he knows about it. The buyer's attitude is nearly passive and his major need is to be informed. Promotion is targeted at:

- Telling the buyer that your product exists.
- Creating an automatic association between the needs area and the product.

Awareness → Interest

This is a movement from a passive stage to an active stage of attention. The buyer will have his curiosity aroused by the product's newness, appearance or concept. His response, however, can be conscious or subconscious. Promotional objectives are:

- To gain his attention through the 'message'.
- To create interest (motivation).
- To provide a succinct summary of the product (information).

Interest → Evaluation

The buyer will consider first the effect of the product upon his personal motivations (life-style, image, etc). Then he will look at the effect on external factors. He will pass through a process of reasoning, analysing the arguments and looking for advantages. Depending upon his needs, he might look for improved efficiency or economy, uniqueness, reassurance or safety. Through promotion, you attempt to:

- Create a situation that encourages the buyer to start this phase of reasoning.
- Discover the buyer's relevant needs.
- Segment and target buyers according to the 'needs' requirements.

Evaluation → Trial

This is a key movement from a mental state of evaluation to a positive action of trial. The buyer's basic requirement is for a suitable opportunity to use the product. Promotional objectives are to:

- Clearly identify usage opportunities.
- Suggest usage when these opportunities occur.

Trial → Usage

The buyer will take this step if his trial has been successful. The objectives of your promotion are to:

- Provide reminders of key elements, such as brand, used areas, advantages, etc.
- Emphasise the success and satisfaction.
- Remind the buyer of usage opportunities and provide supporting proof via third-party references.

Usage → Repeat usage

This is the final objective for promotion. When a buyer moves from occasional usage to constant usage, he will have moved into a state where his selection of your product is automatic. Your objectives are now simpler:

- To maintain the climate that has led to satisfaction.
- Maintain an acceptable image.
- Keep confirming the key qualities of the product.

Each separate promotional technique is concerned with all or part of this process.

Public relations

Unless it is completely invisible, every firm will have an image, but the question is whether it projects the right image. It helps to have a clear idea of how customers see your business at present. This is something that can be researched (see Chapter 3), but of course some information can be obtained by 'keeping one's ear to the ground', although remember, people will often tell you what they think you want to hear. Or worse, you only hear that which confirms your existing view.

The effect of public relations is cumulative and a host of factors, perhaps individually seeming of no major significance, are therefore important. These include the quality of business cards and letter-heads, of switchboard and reception, of brochures, of staff appearance, and so on.

Public relations must provide a planned, deliberate and sustained attempt to promote understanding between you and your public. In fact, not just understanding, but a positive interest in your firm that whets their appetite for more information, prompting enquiries, re-establishes dormant contracts and reinforces your image with existing customers.

Not only is public relations activity potentially a powerful weapon in your promotional armoury, it is also free. Well, at least compared with advertising, which is communication in bought space, but there is a catch. It takes time! And in any small business time is certainly money. Therefore, in too many organisations public relations is neglected because staff are busy, even overstretched, and opportunities are missed. Yet if the power of public relations is consistently ignored, then at worst not only are opportunities missed but the image that occurs by default may actually damage business prospects.

In many ways, therefore, time spent on public relations is time well spent, and often more in terms of relationships rather than resources.

Press relations

Press relations is a very specific form of public relations that can pay dividends, although you must bear in mind that, unlike an advertisement, you cannot guarantee what is going to be said. Having said that, there is no reason to feel that the press will be critical.

Where than do you start? Press releases can be in the form of routine mentions or more particular stories, but remember that much of the impact of both sorts of material is cumulative. Customers will sometimes comment that 'We seem to see mentions of the firm pretty regularly' but have difficulty remembering the exact context of what was said, or more likely written. To achieve this cumulative impact, you need to be constantly on the look-out for opportunities of gaining a mention.

Even routine matters, perhaps the appointment of a new member of staff or a move of offices, may be written up. All that is necessary is, first, to remember to make these announcements, and then to take a disproportionate amount of care and attention as to how they are made. For instance, the announcement of a staff appointment is much more likely to be printed if there is a photograph with it. This takes a little more organising but is well worth the trouble.

Beyond the routine announcement, matters can get a little more difficult. News means exactly that! While it may be of interest to you that the firm has 25 staff, inhabits an eighteenth-century mansion or is reorganising, a journalist will tend to find it difficult to imagine readers starry-eyed with excitement as they read it in his newspaper or journal. You will have to find something with more of an element of news in it; it may be genuinely different, it may be a first comment on something, but it must truly have something of genuine interest about it.

If you become known as a source of good comment, stories and articles, then your press contacts will start to come to you, and the whole process may gain continuity and momentum.

The press release that carries information of the type discussed here is a specialist document, which has to be put together just right, as outlined in Figure 13.

There are two, perhaps conflicting, aspects to putting together a press release that will stand a good chance of publication. The first is to comply with the 'form' demanded by the newspapers, magazines and journals to whom you send your release; the second is to stand out as being of genuine interest from the very large number of releases received.

Take the 'form' first:

- It should carry the words 'Press (or News) release' at the top, together with the date, preferably at the top left hand side of the first page.
- If an embargo is necessary (ie, a request not to publish before a certain date, to ensure news appears as near as possible simultaneously – once an item has been in print others will consider it of less interest) it should be clearly stated 'EMBARGO: not to be published before (time) on (date)'. Underline or use capitals for emphasis.
- Also at the top you need a heading, not too long but long enough to indicate clearly the contents of the release or to generate interest in it.
- Space it out well, wide margins, reasonable gaps between paragraphs and so on. This allows sub-editors to make notes on it.
- If it runs to more than one page make sure it says 'continued' or similar at the foot of the page, even break a sentence at the end of the page.
- Similarly, to make it absolutely clear that there is no more, many put 'end' at the foot of the last page.
- Use newspaper style. Short paragraphs. Short sentences. Two short words rather than one long one.

- Keep it brief, long enough to put over the message and on to a second page if necessary, but no more.
- The first sentences are crucial and need to summarise as far as possible the total message.
- Avoid overt 'plugging' (although that may well be what you are doing). Do not mention names etc right at the beginning, for example.
- Try to stick to facts rather than opinions '. . . this event is being arranged for all those interested in minimising their tax liability' is better than '. . . this event will be of great interest to all those wanting to minimise their tax liability'.
- Opinions can be given, in quotes, and ascribed as such to an individual. This works well and can be linked to the attachment of a photograph (which should be a black and white print and clearly labelled in case it gets separated from the release).
- Do not overdo the use of adjectives, it can jeopardise credibility.
- Avoid underlining things in the text (this is used as an instruction in printing to put words underlined in italics).
- Separate notes to the journal from the text as footnotes, for example, 'photographers will be welcome'; they could get printed as part of the story.
- Never omit from a release, at the end, a clear indication of the person from whom further information can be sought and their telephone number (even if this in on the heading of the first page).
- Make sure, finally, that it is neat, well typed and presentable and that it lists enclosures. Obvious perhaps, but important.

And now, how can you make sure it stands out? Fewer rules exist here, but there are perhaps two:

- Do not 'cry wolf'. Save releases for when you really have a story. If you send a series of contrived ones there is a danger that a good one among them will be ignored.
- Make sure the story sounds interesting and, without overdoing things, be enthusiastic about it. If you are not, why would they be? Perhaps the only good thing in the world that is contagious is enthusiasm.

Figure 13. *Composing a press release* (Reproduced from *The Accountant's Guide to Practice Promotion*, Patrick Forsyth, (Kogan Page 1988)

Perhaps this book itself can provide an example of a release, for the publishers will surely issue such a document to an expectant world (you will, won't you?).

Example 27. Professional press information release

KOGAN PAGE LTD • 120 PENTONVILLE ROAD • LONDON N1 9JN • TEL: 01-278 0433 TLX: 263088 KOGAN G

☐ FOR IMMEDIATE RELEASE

6 January 1989

What's the key to success for every small business?

Marketing.

'What does it involve? Where do I start? What do I do? How do I do it?'

All these questions are answered for the entrepreneur in a new step-by-step guide to marketing:

Making Marketing Work
A Step-by-Step Guide for New Businesses

by Gerard Earls and Patrick Forsyth

New entrepreneurs and people wanting to improve or develop their current business need straightforward, constructive and practical advice. Here it is in a highly accessible form with examples of how the various marketing techniques can contribute to the profitability of the small business.

The book covers all the key marketing activities:

- Market dynamics
- The pricing decision
- Controlling the marketing
- The marketing plan
- The product plan
- Distribution
- Researching the market
- Personal selling and promotion

The authors provide valuable checklists to ensure that the entrepreneur will not omit important stages when carrying out the marketing strategies.

This is a valuable introduction to a vital subject for every small business.

The authors combine the expertise of the academic and the practitioner. Gerard Earls is a senior academic at Middlesex Business School, Hendon. Patrick Forsyth is Client Services Director of Marketing Improvements Ltd.

Both authors are available for interview. Their photographs are enclosed.

Making Marketing Work is published by Kogan Page and is available from all good bookshops or direct from the publisher.

Price: £7.99 paperback

Publication date: 16 March 1989

For further information and review copies, please contact Charles Scott on 01-278 0433.

Advertising

First a definition: Advertising is 'any paid form of non-personal communication directed at target audiences through various media in order to present and promote products, services and ideas'. More simply, it can be called 'salesmanship in print or film'.

The role of advertising, as one of a number of variable elements in the communication mix, is 'to sell or assist the sale of the maximum amount of the product or service, for the minimum cost outlay.'

There is a variety of forms of advertising, depending upon the role it is called upon to play among the other marketing techniques employed, in terms of both the type of advertising and the target to which it is directed. These include, by way of example:

- National advertising
- Retail or local advertising
- Direct mail advertising
- Advertising to obtain leads for sales staff
- Trade advertising
- Industrial advertising.

A more specific way of understanding what advertising can do is to summarise some of the major purposes of advertising – that is, the objectives that can be achieved through using advertising in particular ways. A representative list, which is by no means comprehensive, is as follows:

- to inform potential customers of a new product/service;
- to increase the frequency of use;
- to increase the use of a product/service;
- to increase the quantity purchased;
- to increase the frequency of replacement;
- to lengthen the buying season;
- to present a promotional programme;
- to bring a family of products together;
- to turn a disadvantage into an advantage;
- to attract a new generation of customers;
- to support or influence a franchise dealer, agent or intermediary;
- to reduce brand substitution by maintaining brand loyalty;
- to make known the organisation behind the product/service (corporate image advertising);
- to stimulate enquiries;
- to give reasons why wholesalers and retailers should stock or promote a product;
- to provide technical information about a product/service.

There are clearly many reasons behind the advertising that you see around you. They are not mutually exclusive, of course, and many of those listed apply, or could apply, to your business. Whatever specific objectives the use of advertising seeks to achieve, the main purpose is usually to:

- gain the customer's attention;
- attract customer interest;
- create desire for the product or service; and
- prompt the customer to buy.

Advertising is, therefore, primarily concerned with attitudes and attitude change; creating favourable attributes towards a product or service should be an important part of the advertising effort. Fundamentally, however, advertising also aims to sell, usually with the minimum of delay, although perhaps a longer time period may be needed in the case of informative or corporate (image-building) advertising.

Any advertisement should relate to the product or service, its market and potential market, and, as a communicator, it can perform a variety of tasks. It can:

- Provide information: This information can act as a reminder to current users or it can inform non-users of the product's existence.
- Attempt to persuade: It can attempt to persuade current users to purchase again, non-users to try the product for the first time and new users to change brands or suppliers.
- Create cognitive dissonance: This means advertising can help to create uncertainty about the ability of current suppliers to best satisfy a need. In this way, advertising can effectively persuade customers to try an alternative product or brand. (Extreme versions of this would appear to come under the heading 'knocking copy' – used sometimes by, among others, car manufacturers.)
- Create reinforcement: Advertising can compete with competitors' advertising, which itself aims to create dissonance, to reinforce the idea that current purchases best satisfy the customers' needs.

Moreover, advertising may aim to reduce the uncertainty felt by customers immediately following an important and valuable purchase, when they are debating whether or not they have made the correct choice.

Types of advertising
There are several basic types of advertising and these can be distinguished as follows:

Primary. This aims to stimulate basic demand for a particular product type – for example, insurance, tea or wool.

Selective. This aims to promote an individual brand name, such as a brand of toilet soap or washing powder, which is promoted without particular reference to the manufacturer's identity.

Product. This aims to promote a 'family' branded product or range of related brands where some account must be taken of the image and interrelationship of all products in the mix.

Institutional. This covers public relations-type advertising which, in very general terms, aims to promote the company name, corporate image and the company services.

Advertising media and methods

There is a bewildering array of available advertising media. Here are some of the most popular methods of advertising, with a guide to how they are used:

- Daily newspapers: These often enjoy reader loyalty and, hence, high credibility. Consequently, they are particularly useful for prestige and reminder advertising. As they are read hurriedly by many people, lengthy copy may be wasted.
- Sunday newspapers: These are read at a more leisurely pace and consequently greater detail can be included.
- Colour supplements: These are ideal for advertising, but appeal to a relatively limited audience.
- Magazines: These vary from quarterlies to weeklies and from very general, wide-coverage journals to very specialised interests. Similarly, different magazines of the same type (eg fashion) appeal to different age and socio-economic groups. Magazines are normally colourful and are often read on a regular basis.
- Local newspapers: These are particularly useful for anything local, but are relatively expensive if used for a national campaign. They are sometimes used for test market area advertising support.
- Television: This is regarded as the best overall medium for achieving mass impact and creating an immediate or quick sales response. It is arguable whether or not the audience is captive or receptive, but the fact that television is being used is often sufficient in itself to generate trade support. Television allows the product to be demonstrated and is useful in test marketing new products because of its regional nature, but is very expensive.
- Outdoor advertising: This lacks many of the attributes of press and television but is useful for reminder copy and a support role in a campaign. Strategically placed posters near busy thoroughfares or at commuter stations can offer very effective long-life support advertising.
- Exhibitions: These generate high impact at the time of the exhibition but, except for very specialised ones, their coverage of the potential market is low. They can, however, perform a useful long-term 'prestige' role.
- Cinema: With its escapist atmosphere, this can have an enormous impact on its audience of predominantly young people; but without repetition (ie people visiting the cinema

once every week), it has little lasting effect. It is again useful for backing press and television, but for certain products only, bearing in mind the audience and the atmosphere.

- Commercial radio: Use of this medium for playing popular music to young people offers repetition and has proved an excellent outlet for certain products. It is becoming apparent that the new local radio stations appeal to a wide cross-section of people and thus offer 'support' potential to a wide range of products.
- Direct mail: This offers great flexibility for the advertiser. It is particularly useful for assisting special promotions in certain regions (national coverage of the consumer market being very expensive), and in the industrial and service field where it can be tailored to suit a very specialised audience. Direct mail is so popular in industrial marketing that the major emphasis is on producing a mail shot that is sufficiently different to be noticed and read. The other fundamental problem is the wastage caused by inaccurate and out-of-date mailing lists.

Not all media outlets will be appropriate to the nature of any particular business. Media selection is a complex technical business where professional advice is probably essential. Table 5 (overleaf) illustrates something of the advantages and disadvantages of different media.

Trade advertising
It is often not sufficient to advertise to consumers alone, particularly, where it is important that distributors are willing to stock and promote a product.

Even if the sales force has a prime role to play in ensuring that stocking and promotion objectives are achieved, trade advertising also has an important role to play in this respect:

- It can remind distributors about the product between selling calls.
- It can keep distributors fully informed and up to date on developments and changes of policy.
- It can also alleviate problems associated with the 'cold-call' selling of less well-known products.

Trade advertising is usually confined to specialist trade publications and the use of direct mail communications from the company to its distributors.

Most trade advertising occurs prior to major consumer adver-

Media	Advantages	Disadvantages
National dailies and weeklies	Large circulation; minimum delay before advertisement is published; proofs supplied to enable final advert to be changed or mistakes corrected; specialist staff frequently available to give advice	Typesetting variable in paper set advertisements; expensive; your advertisement competing with large number of others
Local daily evening and weekly newspapers	Attract local people and so avoid waste; costs lower than nationals; minimum delay before publication; act as a guarantee back-up to a national advertisement at little cost	Would not be seen by good prospects outside circulation area
Trade specialist magazines	Usually inexpensive compared with national newspapers; seen by specialist readership if you are only intending to address this group, eg, those in specialist industry	Long delays between each issue (frequently one month); advertisements often not seen by target audience for weeks after publication
Commercial radio and television	Very wide coverage especially at peak listening hours; speed of acceptance of advertisement and broadcast; impact; more people listen to radio and watch television than read newspapers; gain attention of those not necessarily thinking of using/ changing and therefore less likely to notice advertisements in newspapers	Usually very expensive; cost usually means insufficient information can be provided; risk of not being seen or heard by those available during evening or at weekends

Table 5. *Media selection*

tising campaigns to help ensure the buying in of stock in anticipation of future demands to be created by the consumer advertising. Thus, when new products are launched, or special promotions introduced, trade support is often achieved through special offers ('13 for the price of 12') or increased (introductory) discounts, all of which trade advertising can effectively emphasise.

This type of advertising can also communicate to the trade the advantage of new products, as well as the timing and 'weight' of advertising support that is to come.

Presupposing that the analysis of the market has led to a sensible choice of media and advertising strategies, then these have to be communicated to whoever is going to produce the advertisement. At its best, the advertisement strategy statement is brief and economical, and does its job in three paragraphs:

- The basic proposition – the promise to the client, the statement of benefit, to whom.
- The 'reason why' or support proof justifying the proposition, the main purpose of which is to render the proposition as convincing as possible.
- The 'tone of voice' in which the message should be delivered – the image to be projected, and not infrequently the picture the client has of himself/herself, which it could be unwise to disturb, or indeed wise to capitalise on.

In various fields, some of the finest and most effective advertising has sometimes been produced without reference to an 'advertising strategy', or for that matter without knowledge of market facts. However, although research cannot always give all the details, or for that matter always be infallibly interpreted, it can give strong indications and reduce the chances of failure.

Most executives, when faced with a rough or initial visual and copy layout, have an automatic subjective response. 'I like it/I don't like it.' And while the creator may attempt to explain that the appraiser is not a member of the target audience, it is obviously difficult to be objective. Nevertheless, while an attempt at objectivity must be made, there are few experienced advertising or marketing executives who can say that their 'judgement' has never let them down. Advertising remains as much an art as science. The questions that you must ask are:

- Does the advertisement match the strategy laid down?
- Does the advertisement gain attention and create awareness?

- Is it likely to create interest and understanding of the advantages of a particular service?
- Does it create a desire for the benefits and conviction of the need to buy?
- Is it likely to prompt potential clients to action?

In other words: Does the advertising communicate? Will people notice it, understand it, believe it, remember it and buy it? Table 6 summarises the intention and thus 'shape' of a typical advertisement.

Objectives	Methods
Gain customer's attention	Select right media; buy enough space; impact headlines/pictures
Interest reader	Involve customer; make big promises; solve problem; present facts; communicate quality
Make reader desire benefits of your service	Show benefits for them; Don't bore – enthuse; testimonials; message clear and simple; be honest
Get action from reader – make a sale	Summarise benefits; ask reader to buy, call, telephone, attend reception, fill in coupon, make a choice, save time and money, buy now; ask for order

Table 6. *Ingredients of good advertising*

Quoting 'good' advertising is like walking through quicksands. In isolation from its objectives and strategy, its intentions may be unclear. An advert that wins awards may sell little; a simple, unsophisticated one may achieve wonders. So rather than picking and showing a small number of advertisements that might quickly become unrepresentative, the following fictitious example, while somewhat tongue in cheek, is intended to illustrate something of the options in terms of just what an advertisement will use to illustrate and make persuasive its case.

Example 28. A convenience food called '*Splodge*'

As just saying in effect 'here it is' is unlikely to be sufficient, other options must be explored.

- Saying everything about it:

'*Splodge* – the big, wholesome, tasty, non-fattening, instant, easily prepared, chocolate pudding for the whole family'

- Stress one factor, thus implying competitors are weak in this respect:

'*Splodge* – the easily prepared pudding'

Customers may know all puddings of this sort are easy to prepare, but they are still likely to conclude yours is easiest. And if other competitive puddings are being advertised already as 'easily prepared', 'big', 'wholesome' etc what then? You could:

- Pick another factor ignored by your competitors because it is not essential:

'*Splodge* – the pudding in the ring pull pack'

It may be a marginal advantage but your advertisement now implies it is important and that others without it are therefore deficient. Alternatively, you can:

- Pick a characteristic of total irrelevance:

'*Splodge* – the pudding that floats in water'

Or:

- Link it to the pictorial side of the advertisement:

'*Splodge* – the pudding you can eat on the top of a bus'

If competition has done all of this, the you have only one alternative, you must:

- Feature something else in the advertisement, little or nothing to do with the product. This may necessitate repackaging:

'*Splodge* – the only pudding in the *transparent* ring pull pack'

- Or give something away:

'*Splodge*' – the pudding with the *free* sink plunger'

The possibilities are endless, but the ultimate goal is always to make your product appear different and attractive, and desirable because of it.

Sales promotion

In formal marketing terms, sales promotion can be defined as: 'An inducement aimed directly at persuading a specified target audience to achieve one or more defined objectives.' In simpler terms, it is a method of persuading people to take a course of action, which, without that persuasion, they would not normally take.

Sales promotion is an aid to selling, not a substitution for it. It is the tactic that is used because, after careful analysis of the facts and quantification of the objectives, it is likely to prove the most *cost-effective* method of meeting those objectives. You should definitely not resort to sales promotion if:

- all else looks doomed to failure;
- the sales force has a period of inactivity;
- someone thinks it would be nice to have one;
- the chairman's wife had a good idea.

If you attempt to make a problem fit an idea, instead of creating a planned scheme to solve the problem, then experience shows that there is a very great chance that it will not work. Remember that, as with any area of promotion, if it is not precision *planned* and *controlled*, it could well have the directly opposite effect to what you set out to achieve.

The role of sales promotion in marketing

Sales promotion is not an incidental that should only be used as a last minute afterthought, nor should it be left to area sales staff to plan and implement. It is an integral part of the marketing mix, and, as such, requires the same degree of planning as does the mounting of a research project, or the selling-in of a new product. Effective planning is, therefore, essential, whether sales promotion is to be used as a support activity for the company's long-range objectives or as a short-term tactic.

A more specific way of understanding what sales promotion can do for your company is to summarise some of the major purposes of sales promotion, or the objectives that can be achieved through using it effectively in various ways; namely:

- to introduce new products, by motivating customers to try a new product or induce business customers to accept it for resale;
- to attract new customers, by motivating existing customers to try a new product or induce business customers to accept it for resale;
- to maintain competitiveness, by providing preferential discounts or special low prices to enable more competitive

resale prices to be offered;
- to increase sales in off-peak seasons, by encouraging consumption 'out of season';
- to increase trade stocks, by special monetary discounts or quantity purchasing allowances, in return for holding greater than 'normal' levels of stock;
- to induce present customers to buy more, by competitions to encourage customers to think of more ways and more occasions for using the product.

Generally, then, sales promotion is a marketing device to stimulate or restimulate demand for a product, during a particular period. It cannot overcome deficiencies in a product's style, quality, packaging, design or function, but can provide an important addition to advertising activities as an integral part of the communications mix.

Sales promotion types
There are no hard and fast rules for selecting the 'right' sales promotion tactic, since a promotion tactic that is successful in achieving an objective in one industry may not necessarily be successful in achieving a similar objective in another. Similarly, the same promotion tactic might be suitable for meeting different objectives.

In practice, there are likely to be alternative promotion tactics, all of which would be suitable for meeting the same objective. Selection can be assisted by answering the following questions:

- Which promotion tactic best fits the profiles of the target audience?
- What are the advantages of each promotion tactic?
- What are the disadvantages of each promotion tactic?
- Which is likely to give the greatest level of success for the budget available?

The types of promotion tactic currently available are many, and while they cannot be strictly confined into set categories, there are areas where each promotion type stands the greatest chance of achieving a particular defined objective.

Consumer promotions in-home
In-home consumer promotions can help to pre-empt the attempts of competitors to solicit impulse purchases via in-store advertising and display. Techniques used here are:

- sampling, where a sample of the product is delivered free to consumers' homes, say;
- coupon offers via postal and door-to-door distribution, newspaper or magazine distribution, and in-pack/on-pack distribution;
- competitions.

Consumer promotions in-store
Clearly, this type of promotion has the major advantage in that it is featured at the location where the *final* decision to purchase is made. Techniques used here include:

- temporary price reductions;
- extra value offers, including free samples banded on to normal and economy packs;
- premium offers (incentives), including free mail-in premiums, self-liquidating premiums and banded free gifts;
- point-of-sale product demonstrations;
- personality promotions.

Immediate consumer benefit promotions
Here, consumer reward for purchasing is immediate, and, as with most incentives, the sooner the reward can be expected and received after the qualifying action, the greater will be the positive effects of that incentive in stimulating purchase action. Included in this promotion category are:

- price reductions
- free gifts
- banded pack offers
- economy packs.

Consumer promotions by distributors
These include the following:

- special trade-in prices for used goods;
- free gifts, such as an electric food mixer with a refrigerator;
- trading stamps or gift vouchers;
- mail-order promotions, such as special prices or credit terms.

Trade promotions
Reasons for promoting to the trade:

- to obtain support and co-operation in stocking and promoting

products to customers;
- to induce distributors to increase their stock levels, where research may have revealed lower than average stockholdings;
- to pre-empt competitive selling activities by increasing trade stocks.

Techniques used in trade promotion:

Bonusing. This can take the form of monetary discounts or 'free goods' ('13 cases for the price of 12'), or special quantity rate terms.

Incentive schemes. These can be tailored to the needs of a distributor's sales force. Alternatively, annual, or promotional, sales targets may be set and agreed with distributors, and extra cash incentives paid according to the extent to which sales exceed the target. May also include competitions, particularly for sales staff.

Dealer loaders. Instead of money, gift incentives may be offered to distributors, or their salesforce, for achieving agreed sales targets or stocking certain quantities of product.

Thus, it can be seen that trade promotion can be an extremely important element within the total market strategy in helping to ensure that stocks are available in the right distribution channels and at the right time.

Co-operative advertising schemes. Assistance with preparation of advertisements or media costs.

Provision of display materials. Either free of charge or on a shared cost basis.

Tailor-made promotions. Custom designed to the outlet's individual requirements often promoting their own name and corporate image.

Industrial promotions
Until recently, sales promotion has been almost the exclusive domain of consumer goods markets, probably because of a certain conservative attitude within many industrial companies. This atitude is outmoded, as many of the problems that sales promotion schemes can be really effective in alleviating, present themselves in equal measure to both industrial and consumer goods firms.

The reasons for promoting to industry include the following:

- to encourage repeat purchase;
- to secure marginal buyers;
- to meet competition;
- to ensure that bills are paid on time;
- to stimulate a sales force or a dealer or agency network;
- to induce rapid market penetration when launching a new product;
- to sustain perception of value over and above that intrinsically possessed by the product itself;
- to reduce the perceived risk involved in buying expensive and long-lasting items of equipment;
- to smooth out costly buying cycles.

All are problems solved by motivating customers to behave slightly more in line with the interests of the selling organisation so that it, in turn, can become socially and economically more efficient.

The techniques used in industrial promotion include:

- *Price-off promotions*: Special terms for specific customers at specific times.
- *Couponing*: Coupons entitling the holder to special terms.
- *Competitions*: Prizes awarded to sales staff or middlemen for achieving pre-set objectives.
- *Loyalty schemes*: Give-away to loyal customers, £50 off next purchase.
- *Reciprocal trading schemes*: Guaranteeing to a customer that your organisation will in turn buy his product.
- *Credit schemes*: Leasing, consignment schemes or delayed invoicing.
- *Premium offers*: Special 'linked product' package deals ('13 for 12' offers) or free spares.
- *Trade-in allowances*: Special terms for trading in a competitive or obsolete model.
- *Guarantees*: Extra special guarantees for specific risky products.
- *Sampling*: Distributing trial offers of a product, free demonstrations of trial installations.
- *Co-operative advertising*: Allowance given for dealer advertising featuring a specified product.
- *Training schemes*: Free training for operatives or middlemen.
- *Container premiums*: Products distributed in a free multi-use container.

- *Full-range buying schemes*: Special terms for across-the-range orders.
- *Co-operative promotions*: Offering a range of products and services as a 'system' with the help of complementary suppliers.

How to promote (industrial) products

It must be stated immediately that the following approach and considerations are not confined to industrial goods only. Industrial products have been chosen to illustrate that not only are industrial promotions available (see previous section), but also that there is a practical way of combating industrial competition, other than through cutting price, and also a systematic approach to developing such promotions.

What distinguishes consumer from industrial goods firms is not only the nature of the product but, more importantly, its destination. Industrial goods are sold to other organisations (ie, derived demand), and they are not always distinguishable from consumer goods, for example, cars, typewriters, fuel, nuts and bolts, clothing, stationery, etc are sold to both.

Of course, at the other end of the size scale, the product differs substantially, but there it forms the minority of transactions, however important each one is individually. Having established the importance of the destination in categorising an industrial product, let us now look at the significance of that destination in determining the nature of the appropriate sales promotion. This can be illustrated by considering various situations and recognising that in practice there is often considerable interaction between them. Each situation, however, requires validation before it can be accepted as an accurate representation of your industrial marketing situation.

The more discretion a buyer has over choice of product or supplier, the more his buying behaviour will approximate to that of the consumer
(The 'buyer' is a person who has most influence over the nature, size, direction and timing of an order, and may be a group of key people.) In such a situation it becomes possible to transfer the use of promotional schemes, suitably modified in terms of content to solve a particular industrial problem, straight across from consumer to industrial marketing.

The more discretion a buyer possesses, the more open he is likely to be to what can be termed 'idiosyncratic' as opposed to 'organisationally' directed buying behaviour. Factors that may affect the amount of discretion possessed by an industrial buyer are:

- degree of power possessed (the more power, the more discretion);
- length of time successfully served as the buyer;
- uniqueness of the contribution made to the firm's success;
- routineness of the task;
- organisational philosophy of the firm (given the level in the hierarchy at which an order is customarily placed; the more decentralised, the more discretion);
- pressures on the need to buy.

By considering criteria such as these, you could completely reappraise your promotional approach, so as to bring it more into line with consumer goods practices.

The larger the deal, up to a point, the more the appeals of the promotion should be aimed at increasing the monetary value of that deal, and at guaranteeing performance.
At very high order values, status, prestige, vagaries of high technology and politics begin to play a dominant part in the purchase decision. Orders can be swung by diplomatic pressure on, say, the chief executive or by the opportunity for reciprocal trading, for example. It is assumed, however, that between low and high value deals the 'economic' or 'budgetary motive' prevails for deciding the terms of the deal. As long as the customer organisation believes this to be true, and as long as it insists that buying decisions at middle value order levels are best made by several people, then the seller is forced to offer promotional schemes emphasising 'value for money'; for example, cost reduction schemes, guaranteed delivery performance and quality control standards. Other schemes may be acceptable, but only if they legitimately help the buying group as a whole to achieve its objectives.

The more standardised the product and the more generalised the statements it is possible to make about the problems it solves in use, the more generalised can the promotional proposition be
This is obviously logical, but it does illustrate how you can determine the 'precision' of promotional offers you make, and thus, for example, the best way of communicating them; for example, through the media or the sales force, to take two extremes.

The longer the time-span over which a buyer is committed to a product, the more must promotions be aimed at reducing perceived risk
This is of paramount importance for products sold at the design stage, perhaps years before commissioning or consumption.

Risks grow exponentially, especially in the buyer's mind, with the passage of time because of:

- increasing difficulty of profit forecasting;
- technological risks of malperformance;
- obsolescence;
- misuse in the hands of inexperienced operatives and managers.

These dangers can be alleviated by the imaginative use of promotional schemes, such as:

- free consultancy, advice and training;
- guaranteed buy-back terms;
- a financing or leasing scheme based upon revenue-earning capacity over time, rather than on a cost-incurring basis;
- a suitably negotiated insurance deal to all customers at premiums lower than each one would obtain separately;
- an effective technical and service back-up facility;
- trial installations.

The more similar industrial products are to consumer goods, the more schemes, customarily used by consumer durable goods manufacturers, can be transferred to industrial markets
The similarities are as follows:

- similar purchase behaviour;
- both are often bought repeatedly, although the purchase interval can be longer for some;
- both are frequently sold through middlemen;
- both require financing, service, guarantee, insurance and 'linked' package deals;
- both need special attention at their launching;
- both are sold through a sales force who themselves need motivation and support.

In this way, and using these illustrative situations as a guide, any industrial organisation can begin to widen its effective choice of sales promotions, away from the rather overused and stilted panic price reduction, and based on adaptations from consumer goods promotions.

The creative factor

With the ever-increasing number of promotions, it is becoming difficult to be original. Many promotions fail because they say nothing more to the target audience than:

'Everybody else offered this and did all right, so I thought I would try it.'

Originality and creativity are two very important aspects for a successful promotion. A very creative and original scheme, even though inexpensive, can, and often does, score over a high budget, stereotyped uncreative promotion.

So, when developing promotions, investigate what promotions have been run in the area you intend attacking and make a determined attempt to introduce a new creative concept. If this fails, then investigate new angles on an existing concept. If you fail in both, and can still justify the promotion in relation to the objectives, then proceed.

Conclusions

Sales promotion involves the making of special offers with a specific time limit to persuade a specified target audience to achieve one or more defined objectives. Thus it can be used to:

- introduce new products
- attract new customers
- maintain competitiveness
- increase sales in off-peak seasons
- increase trade stocks
- induce present customers to buy more.

There is a vast array of sales promotion methods that can be broadly grouped as follows:

- consumer promotions
- trade promotions
- industrial promotions.

In promoting industrial products, much can be adapted from consumer marketing and effectively applied in industrial markets.

Now, having reviewed something of the techniques, we can turn to how to use them.

The promotional plan

The preparation and implementation of a comprehensive promotional strategy necessitates systematic planning. The checklist below makes clear the 12 key points involved:

- Analyse the market and clearly identify the exact need.
- Ensure the need is real and not imaginary, and that support is necessary.
- Establish that the tactics you intend to adopt are likely to be the most cost-effective.
- Define clear and precise objectives.
- Analyse the tactics available, taking into consideration the key factors regarding:
  - the market
  - the target audience
  - the product/service offered
  - the company organisation/resources.
- Select the mix of tactics you will use.
- Check your budget to ensure funds are available.
- Prepare a written operation plan.
- Discuss and agree the operation plan with all concerned and obtain management decision to proceed.
- Communicate the details of the campaign to whoever is implementing it and ensure that they fully understand what they must do, and when.
- Implement the campaign, ensuring continuous feedback of necessary information for monitoring performance.
- Analyse the results, showing exactly what has happened, what factors affected the result (if any) and how much the campaign cost.

These can then be examined in more detail under five main sequential headings.

Analysis of the need

The prime difficulty in the analysis stage is not so much the identification of the need, but ensuring that the need is real and not imaginary.

Identification of a need can come from:

- formal research
- your own company investigation
- sales staff

- specific market demands
- your own observations.

In such an analysis, you are looking at the interrelation of customer categories, products and types of business. For example, a small travel agent might look at:

Customers: Families, individuals, companies, etc
Products: Holidays, air tickets, car hire, etc
Business: New business (first time buyer), repeat business
                (past customer buying again and more)

He may then have to plan different promotional activities to impact specific individual areas of business, possibly to increase long distance holiday purchases by retired couples.

Once a need has been clearly identified, it must be established that whatever support you intend using is likely to be the most cost-effective method of fulfilling that need. Then the planning stage can commence.

Preparing the operation plan
The first stage of any planning must be the quantification of the objectives. A clear statement of exactly what you want to achieve, stated as specifically as possible, is needed. For the travel agent, an objective that says 'to improve sales of holidays' is just not precise enough, whereas an objective that states 'to improve the sales of long distance holidays to retired couples by 50 per cent this year' makes it clear to everyone exactly what needs to be done, and above all, how success will be measured.

Once the objective is finalised the selection of tactics can take place, which will depend on a number of factors:

The market
- What is its nature?
- Is it buoyant or in a low period?
- Is it price conscious? If so, how?
- What is the competition doing?
- What is the audience profile?

The target audience
- What are the types of people?
- What are their buying habits?
- What motivates buyers?
- What promotion are they already known to accept or reject?

The product/service
- What is its current performance?
- What are its strengths and weaknesses?
- What promotional support has it received in the past?
- What is the supply availability?
- What is the market profile/image?
- What is the position in the product life cycle?

Company organisation
- What are your current sales and promotional methods?
- Would some tactics cause internal difficulties in terms of administration, for example?
- Is the company involved in any other activity that might affect what you want to do, or detract from it?

In considering this analysis phase you could usefully read again Chapter 4 on marketing planning. In addition, Example 29 (overleaf) provides guidance on setting the budget.

Having answered these questions, there may be a number of alternative tactics, all of which would be suitable for achieving the objective. The decision as to which to use will then depend on which is the most cost-effective.

Once the decision on tactics has been made, the details should be formalised into a written operation plan. It is always worth writing this down, even in a small business. It is not a one-off exercise but will eventually provide a reference document which, if updated regularly, will help to develop the plan for the next period. It should include:

- background information as to why the promotional support is necessary;
- the objectives;
- a profile of the target audience;
- reference to product details;
- details of additional support other than that which you are actually planning – perhaps that being done by the trade;
- budget details showing how much the action is estimated to cost;
- implementation details showing exactly how the plan will be implemented;
- controls, standards and methods of obtaining results;
- an action plan, or timetable, showing what actions are required, when they should be carried out and by whom.

Example 29. Some approaches for deciding the budget

Percentage of sales. To take a fixed percentage based usually on forecast sales relies on the questionable assumption that there is always a direct relationship between promotional expenditure and sales. It assumes, for example, that if increased sales of 10 per cent are forecast, a 10 per cent increase in promotional effort will also be required. This may or may not be realistic and depends on many external factors. Although this is the most traditional and easiest approach, it is probably the least effective.

Competitive parity approach. This involves spending the same amount as the competition, or maintaining a proportional expenditure of total industry appropriation or an identical percentage of gross sales revenue compared with competitive firms. The assumption is that market share will, in this way, be maintained. But competition may be aiming at a slightly different sector, and including competition in the broadest sense (carpets/cars) is no help. If you can form a view of competitive/industry activity, it may be useful, but the danger of this approach is that competitors' spending represents the 'collective wisdom' of an industry, and the blind may be leading the blind!

It is important to remember that competitive expenditure cannot be more than an indication of the budget that should be established. In terms of strategy, it is entirely possible that expenditure should be considerably greater than a competitor – to drive him out – or perhaps for other reasons a lot less.

Remember that no two companies pursue identical objectives from an identical base line of resources, market standing, etc, and that it is fallacious to assume that all competitors will spend equal or proportional amounts of money with exactly the same level of efficiency.

What-can-you-afford approach. This method appears to be based on the premise that if spending something is right, but you cannot objectively decide the optimum amount, whatever money is available will do.

The factors you should consider are:

- What is available after all the other costs (premises, staff, selling expenses, etc) have been accounted for?
- The cash situation in the business as a whole
- The revenue forecast.

Then in many companies, advertising and sales promotion are left to share out the tail-end of the budget. More expenditure is considered to be analogous with lower profits; in others, more expenditure on advertising leads to more sales at marginal cost, which in turn leads to higher overall profits.

Fixed sum per sales unit. This is similar to the percentage of sales approach, except that a specific amount per unit (say, per holiday sold) is used rather than a percentage of pound sales value. In this way, money for promotional purposes is not affected by changes in price. This takes an enlightened view that advertising expenditure is an investment, not merely a cost.

What have you learned from previous years? The best predictor for next year's budget is this year's. Are results as you predicted? What relationship has your spending to competition? What is happening in the market? What effect is it having and what effect is it likely to have in future? To try and answer such questions you can:

- experiment in a controlled area to see whether you are under- or overspending. As the chairman of Unilever once said: 'I know that 50 per cent of our advertising expenditure is wasted, the trouble is I don't know which 50 per cent.'
- monitor results, which is relatively easy, and use the results of experiments with different budget levels in planning the next ones, although you must always bear in mind that all other things do not remain equal.

Task method approach. Recognising the weaknesses in other approaches, a more comprehensive four-step procedure is possible. Emphasis here is on those tasks involved in the process and already described in relation to constructing a promotional strategy. The four steps of this method are:

- *Analysis*: Make an analysis of the marketing situation to uncover the factual basis for the promotional approach. Marketing opportunities and specific marketing targets for strategic development should also be identified.
- *Determine objectives*: From the analysis, set clear short- and long-term promotional objectives for continuity and 'build up' of advertising impact and effect.
- *Identify the promotional tasks*: Determine the promotional activities required to achieve the marketing and promotional objectives.
- *'Cost out' the promotional tasks*: What is the likely cost of each element in the communications mix and the cost effectiveness of each element? What medium is likely to be chosen and what is the target (ie, number of advertisements, point-of-sale material, sales promotions, direct mail leaflets, etc)? In advertising, the media schedule can be easily converted into an advertising budget by adding space or time costs to the cost of preparing advertising material. The sales promotional budget is usually determined by costing out the expenses of preparing and distributing sales promotion material, etc.

The great advantage of this budgetary approach compared with others is that it is comprehensive, systematic and likely to be more realistic. However, other methods can still be used to provide 'ball-park' estimates, although such methods can produce disparate answers, as follows:

- we can afford £10,000;

- the task requires £15,000;
- to match competition requires £17,500;
- last year's spending was £8,500.

The decision than becomes a matter of judgement, allowing for your overall philosophy and objectives.

There is no wholly accurate mathematical or automatic method of determining the promotional budget. The task method does provide, if not the easiest, then probably the most accurate method of determining what your promotional budget should be.

Pre-launch preparation

Provided the operation plan has been correctly prepared, the pre-launch preparation should be a formality. But this can only be achieved if the operation plan has been discussed and agreed with everyone connected with the support activity, well before any action is required. This will ensure that you pick up ideas, or identify snags, from everyone in the business, some of whom may surprise you with their constructive comments. Do not forget that if people feel involved, they will be more easily committed to the next stage.

Implementation

The success or failure of any promotional activity, provided it has been thoroughly planned, then rests on how well it is implemented. The effectiveness of the implementation depends on how well the details are communicated and controlled.

The details of what is to be done must be communicated in such a way that they are clearly understood by everyone.

Effective methods of controlling the implementation must be set up to obtain maximum feedback while promotional activity is running. This will permit necessary changes to be made at the earliest opportunity.

The post-analysis of results

Advertising, sales promotion and merchandising campaigns usually involve a great deal of personnel time and are often expensive. It is therefore, important to know how much money is being spent, and what achievements are obtained from that expenditure.

Examing the detailed results of every form of promotional activity will show clearly:

- what the situation was prior to the activity;

- what you were trying to achieve (the objective);
- what the situation was after the promotional activity had ended (what was achieved);
- whether your objectives were entirely met, and if not, why not;
- whether there were any factors outside your control which might have influenced the result, what they were and their effect;
- what has happened to the rest of the market or at least to your near competitors;
- what the effect might have been had you not carried out the promotion;
- what the budget was and how it was spent.

Careful analysis of what has been achieved is important, not least as part of the planning and consideration of what to do next, which should be occurring in a continuing cycle.

No promotional activity you plan can be carried out in isolation – promotion involves everything. Any business must be truly customer orientated. Only if the service elements are, together, of the right level will final conversion to purchase occur (see Figure 14). The best promotional plan you can conceive will fail if any other key element in the chain is inadequate; for example:

People. Any of your employees with customer contact duties are the final link in the chain. Do they really complete that link correctly? Are they really selling, not just providing information? What is the quality of the letters they send? Are customers impressed with the response when they telephone you? And do you know these things? When did you last telephone your own offices incognito to see how customers are really dealt with?

Business methods. The systems and procedures you use also need to be geared to what is right for the customer. Are your procedures simple, straightforward and understandable to the customer? Are these, and perhaps the mass of other technical matters of the business, explained to them? Or is there a danger that methods and practices are not tailored to helping the customer, but have grown up haphazardly over the years for no good reason?

Once the promotional activity has brought prospective customers to your door, all the other resources at your disposal must be actively geared to converting them into actual purchasers. Sometimes these seem designed to prevent or ignore the final step rather than to increase the danger of making a sale! The customer will do business with you only if he feels, or rather if you

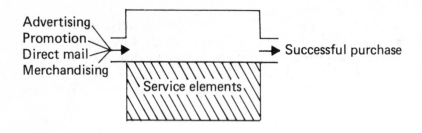

Figure 14. *Conversion to sales by correct service*

persuade him, that you will provide for him better than the alternatives will.

Planning and implementing a soundly based systematic promotional plan for a business is not easy. Nor is ensuring that all the back-up resources, people, skills and systems are geared to converting the initial enthusiasm created in potential customers into actual business. It is certainly necessary, and done successfully, provides a sound basis for securing and, more important, expanding the business you do.

Checklist

- Have you reviewed the range of promotional techniques available, their respective roles and appropriateness for your business?
- Do you have a promotional plan?
- Do you have a planned budget? Is it the result of analysis? Is it in writing?
- Do you review regularly against the plan for additional promotional opportunites (for example, in PR)?
- Is implementation of the planned activities allocated to appropriate people inside or outside the company?
- Are you ready if your promotion works? Are your systems, methods and people able to cope appropriately with the incoming enquiries and the service aspects of the business? Do you check these standards regularly?
- Overall, is what you do sufficiently creative to differentiate your product/service from competitors?

9
Personal Selling

Personal selling means simply 'one-to-one' persuasive communication. But there is more to it than that. In most businesses, you must find customers, persuade them, then maintain and develop their interest on a regular basis. Sometimes, and in some businesses, you must initiate contact; at other times or in other businesses, they contact you. Selling is bound up with customer service and involves systems, to make sure it occurs, as well as techniques to make the process persuasive.

Indeed, selling involves the simplest situations. For example, an off licence may be able to increase sales significantly just by ensuring that every time a member of staff is asked for spirits, they ask, 'How many mixers do you want?' Many people will respond positively to what has been called the 'gin and tonic' effect, the linking of one product with another. Sometimes the question is even simpler: the waiter in a hotel or bar, for example, who asks 'Another drink?'

At the other end of the scale, sales do not come from the single isolated success of one interaction with the customer. A chain of events may be involved, several people, a long period of time and, importantly, a cummulative effect. In other words, each stage, perhaps involving some combination of meetings, proposals, presentations, and more meetings, must go well or you do not move on to the next.

So with the thought in mind that the detail of what is necessary will vary depending on circumstances, let us review the stages in turn and some of the principles involved.

Identifying prospects

To take the initiative in approaching people, it is necessary to identify prospects (potential customers) as accurately as possible, otherwise time, and therefore money, may be wasted. Sources of information about customers will vary depending on who you are selling to; an example will highlight the principles.

Example 30. Identifying prospects

Walter has a successful retail travel agency business. He identifies that, in addition to selling to customers over the counter, he is well placed to deal with commercial accounts in the area in which his business is located. He needs to initiate some contacts, but with whom? The first stage is to check. He looks at his files, companies he has dealt with previously and individual customers who work for the right kind of company. This produces some names but he needs more and considers a list of sources including:

- Local Chambers of Commerce and Trade: Not just by consulting their lists but perhaps by belonging to them or addressing their meetings;
- public libraries: Particularly as a source of some of the items mentioned later in this list;
- his suppliers: Among the companies he buys from, such as office equipment and supplies, there may be potential customers;
- credit bureaux or other professional service agents;
- personal observation: The factory down the road, the new office block on the corner;
- local government offices;
- referrals, existing customers, suppliers' customers, contacts or friends;
- his bank;
- mailing lists: Often available for rent as well as from directories;
- exhibitions and trade promotion events;
- local hotels who already receive business from him and may be helpful in return. What meetings or exhibitions go on there?
- company annual reports (from his public library);
- company house/employee magazines (from his public library);
- trade/industry/technical journals (from his public library);
- directories of companies (from his public library);
- telephone directories/yellow pages (from his public library).

One or a combination of these can supply valuable information about prospects: the names of companies, what business they are in, if it is going well or badly, whether they export, how big they are, who owns them, what subsidiaries or associates they have and, last, but certainly not least, who runs and manages them.

Exactly which individual is then approached is obviously vital, and may not be a simple decision. Indeed, it may be that more than one person is involved. For example, the person who travels, the person who sends him, the person who pays and perhaps also the person who makes the booking. There is many a secretary with considerable discretionary power in making bookings, and not least among their considerations will be how straightforward and easy the travel agency is for them to deal with personally.

As well as considering which individual to approach, the other important assessment at this stage is that of financial potential. How much business might be obtained from them in, say, a year? This analysis will rule out some prospects as not being worth further pursuit. Experience will sharpen the accuracy with which these decisions can be made, but meantime a good first list is developing.

The old military maxim that 'time spent in reconnaissance is seldom wasted' is a good one. In war it can help to prevent casualties. In business it not only produces information on who should be contacted, but provides a platform for a more accurately conceived, and more successful, approach.

So having identified who will be contacted, his next step is *organising the approach*. A number of factors may be important here, both before an approach is made and in follow-up. Two key areas he needs to consider before making an approach are:

- How will the approach be made?

The ultimate objective is almost certainly a face-to-face meeting, which must be held before any substantial business can result. Such a meeting can be set up by:

- 'cold calling', that is, calling without an appointment;
- sending a letter or card with or without supporting literature;
- telephoning 'cold' or as follow-up to a letter or promotion;
- getting people together, initially as a group, and making a presentation at your premises, a hotel or other venue, or through a third party, (such as at a Chamber of Trade meeting).

The logistics are also important. What is needed is a campaign spread over time so that if and when favourable responses occur they can be followed up promptly; such responses may be more difficult to cope with if they all occur together.

The next consideration is:

- Who will make the approach?

The process will almost certainly involve approaching, meeting and discussing matters with people senior in, and knowledgeable about, their own business. The approach therefore needs to be made by people with the right profile, who will be perceived as being appropriate, and who can really give an impression of competence. They will also need to have the right attitude, wanting to win business in what may be a new and perhaps more difficult area. And they need the knowledge and skills to tackle the task in hand: knowledge of the customers, the agency and its services, of overseas places and processes or the ability to find out quickly. Detail is important. The export manager who is made late for an appointment will be equally upset whether he has missed a flight connection or simply been misinformed on the time it takes to get from airport to hotel. The travel agent, rightly or wrongly, will probably get the blame. Finally, skills in customer contact, selling and negotiation are needed as well as in all those areas, such as writing sales letters, involved in making the approach. Making the right choice of person is therefore crucial and in the long term, a small company set on developing its business travel side may need to consider recruitment, training or both.

The initial approach is vital, like any first impression, and it may be very difficult having received an initial negative response to organise a second chance. Having thought the process through in this way, the chances of success are that much greater.

Whatever the kind of customers you seek, if an individual approach is necessary and you need more prospects than can economically be found by promotional activity, then such a process of analysis and action will be necessary. Once contact occurs, then whoever takes on the role of sales person must understand the sales process and use that knowledge in a way that makes the sales contact both persuasive and yet always acceptable to other people, in this case the prospects involved.

The sales process

The sales person who does not understand a buyer has a hard job selling anything, and the selling sequence cannot be followed or appreciated properly without understanding the buying process. You cannot sell without understanding how and why people buy. In a small comapny where many will have outside contact with people who are at some stage of the buying process, this understanding of buying is very important.

Many involved with, indeed starting, a small business come from an administrative or technical, rather than selling background, and as a result there is often an element of apprehension about having a selling role. But by understanding the buying process, and seeing its connection with selling, you can see that many beliefs about selling ability are frequently myths, and that magical talents are not needed in order to be a satisfactory seller.

The process of selling cannot take place without communication, and that requires two people: the buyer and the seller. As in all communications, little is achieved if one does not understand the other. Let us therefore look first at the buyer.

The buying process, which governs the buyer, can be broken down into seven stages through which the buying mind goes on its way to reach a decision. These stages are the following:

- I am important and I want to be respected.
- Consider my needs.
- How will your ideas help me?

- What are the facts?
- What are the snags?
- What shall I do?
- I approve.

Any sales attempt that responds unsatisfactorily to any of these stages is unlikely to end in an order. The buying mind has to be satisfied on each point before moving to the next, and to be successful a sales presentation sequence must match the buying sequence, and run parallel to it.

Table 7 shows the buying process alongside the sales objectives, what you are trying to achieve at each stage, and the technique employed in any sales communication. The two keys to success are the process of matching the buyer's progression and describing, selectively, the product, and discussing it in a way that relates to precisely what the buyer needs. This may be a little different to the way 'product knowledge' is generally organised for you, which is therefore examined in the next section.

How people buy	Sales objective	How to sell: Sales technique
I am important Consider my needs	To explore and identify customer's needs	Opening the sales interview
How will your ideas help me? What are the facts?	To select and present the benefits that satisfy the customer's needs	The sales presentation
What are the snags?	To prevent, by anticipating, snags likely to arise or handle objections raised so that the customer is satisfied with the answers	Handling sales objections
What shall I do? I approve	To obtain a buying decision from the customer or a commitment to the proposition presented	Closing the sale

Table 7. *The buying sequence*

In all successful sales, the buyer and the seller would have gone through this sequence stage by stage. If the attempt to sell, which just as often begins with an attempt to buy, is unsuccessful, it will be found that:

- the sequence has not taken place at all;

- some stage has been missed out;
- the sequence has been followed too quickly or too slowly, which means the seller has allowed it to get out of step with the buying process.

Early on, because the customer needs to go through other stages, you may not always be able to aim for a commitment to buy, but you must have a clear objective on which to 'close' in mind. This may be to get the customer to allow you to send literature, to fix an appointment for a representative to call or to provide sufficient information for a detailed quotation to be prepared. Whatever your objective is, however, it is important to know and be able to recognise the various stages ahead. With any customer contact (by telephone or letter as well as face to face), you can identify:

- What stage has been reached in the buying process.
- Whether your selling sequence matches it.
- If not, why not?
- What do you need to do if the sequence does not match.
- Has a step been missed?
- Are you going too fast?
- Should you go back in the sequence?
- Can your objectives still be achieved, or were they the wrong objectives?
- How can you help the buyer through the rest of the buying process?

Naturally, the whole buying process is not always covered in only one contact between the company and the customer. Every phone call does not result in a sale, and neither does it result in a lost sale. Some stages of the selling sequence have to be followed up in each sales contact, but the logic applies equally to a series of calls which form the whole sales approach to each customer. For a doubtful customer, or a sale of great complexity and expense, there may be numerous contacts to cover just one of the stages before the buyer is satisfied and both can move on to the next stage. Each call or contact has a selling sequence of its own in reaching the call objectives. Each call is a part of an overall selling sequence aimed at reaching overall sales objectives.

Planning the selling sequence is therefore as much a part of call planning as it is of sales planning, but only rarely does a call take place exactly as planned. Knowing and using the sales sequence, and being able to recognise stages of the buying process, are, however, invaluable if you are to realise your potential for direct sales results. Thus everyone needs to be able to deal effectively with all calls and pass on those that will be completed by others, such as the sales person, in the organisation.

With this basic appreciation of the buyer, and what is directing his reactions, we can look closer at the key areas of the sales approach.

Using product information effectively

Identifying with the buyer, in order to recognise the stages of the buying process and to match them with a parallel selling sequence, must extend to the presentation of the sales proposition. Nowhere is this more important than in the way you look at the product, or service, which you are selling.

Product knowledge is too often taken for granted by companies and sales people. Sadly, experience of hearing hundreds of sales people talking unintelligible gibberish does not support this complacency. Sales people are usually given inadequate product knowledge and what is given is slanted towards the company, not the customer. Managers are often still heard to say proudly, 'Everyone joining us spends six months in the factory, to learn the business', but many then emerge with no better idea of what the product means to the customer. Everyone with any role to play in sales-oriented customer contact must consider the product, and all that goes with it, from the customers' point of view. In a small company, this means rapid, precise and appropriate briefing for all staff involved in the sales process.

- Don't sell products, sell benefits.

If you get into the habit of seeing things through the customer's eyes, you will realise that you do not sell special promotions, 'free' trial offers or fancy wrappings. You do not really sell products either. You sell what customers want to buy and:

- Customers don't buy promotions or products, they buy benefits.

But what are benefits? Benefits are what products, promotions or services do for the customer. It is not as important what the products are, as what they do or mean to the customer.

For example, a person does not buy an electric drill because he wants an electric drill, but because he wants to be able to make holes. He buys holes, not a drill. He buys the drill for what it will do (make holes). And this in turn may only be important to him because of a need for storage and a requirement to put up shelving.

When you realise this, your selling becomes more effective and also easier. You do not have to try to sell the same product to a lot of different people, but you meet each person's needs with personal benefits.

Benefits are what the things you sell can do for each individual customer – the things he wants them to do for him. Different customers buy the same product for different reasons. Therefore, you must identify and use the particular benefits of interest to them.

- What a product 'is' is represented by its 'features'.
- What a product 'does' is described by its 'benefits'.

If forgotten, then the things that are important to a customer will not always be seen as important from the seller's viewpoint, particularly if he has had little or no sales training. The result can, understandably, end up in a conflict of priorities, as shown in Table 8.

Customer	**Salesman**
Himself: Satisfaction of his needs, eg mortgage to buy a house, new machine to increase production	*Himself:* His company, his products, his ideas
His needs and the benefits that satisfy them	*His product* and making this customer buy it
This salesman: Salesman's company, salesman's products, salesman's ideas	*Benefits* to this customer
Buying from this salesman	*Customer's needs:* Benefits that satisfy this customer's needs

Table 8. *Differing viewpoints of seller/customer*

The customer is most unlikely to see things from the seller's point of view. Everyone is to himself the most important person in the world. Therefore, to be successful, the seller has to be able to see things from the customer's point of view and demonstrate through his words and actions that he has done so. His chances of success are greater if he can understand the needs of the people he talks to and make them realise that he can help them to fulfil those needs.

You achieve this essentially by the correct use of benefits. In presenting any proposition to a customer, even simply recommending a product in reply to a query, you should always translate what you are offering into what it will do.

Often, a company, and the people who write the sales literature, grow product-orientated, and gradual product development can reinforce this attitude by adding more and more features. It is only a small step before everyone is busy trying to sell the product on its features alone. It is interesting to note that often, when this happens, advertising and selling become more and more forceful, with the features being given a frantic push, as passing time reveals that there has been no great rush to buy.

Two examples over the past years, familiar to everyone, are the audio and camera markets. Stereo equipment, in particular, is almost always promoted on features only. Masses of technical terms, most of them meaningless to the majority of end-users, dominate advertisements and brochures, while the visual communication is based entirely on the appearance of the amplifier, speakers or turntable. Yet what people want from a stereo set is sound and reliability – years of listening pleasure.

When competitive products become almost identical in their performance, it can be difficult to sell benefits, since all seem to offer the same benefits. Choice then often depends on the personal appeal of some secondary feature. But even then, there must be emphasis on the benefits in those features, rather than on the features themselves. In 'industrial' selling (to other companies rather than to individual consumers), it is more important than ever to concentrate on benefits rather than on features, which may be little better than gimmicks. Features are only important if they support benefits that the customer is interested in.

Deciding to concentrate on benefits is only half the battle, however. They have to be the right benefits. In fact, benefits are only important to a customer if they describe the satisfaction of his needs. Working out the needs, and then the benefits, means being 'in the customers' shoes'.

● Who is the customer, what are his needs?

To know what benefits to put forward, you must know what the customers' needs are. And to know them, you have to know exactly who the customer is. Very often, the customer you deal with is the user – the person who will actually use the product. But frequently, the direct customer is a purchaser or a decision-maker, who is not the user. This is most common in industrial selling, when a buying department is often responsible for ordering as well as handling the purchasing of most of a company's requirements. In consumer products, a manufacturer may sell to a wholesaler, the wholesaler to retailer, and it is only the retailer who actually sells to the users.

Naturally, the requirements of the end-user will also be of interest to the various intermediaries, but the best results are going to be obtained if you can bear in mind the needs of both the buyer and the user, and the differences between their various needs.

To do this, it is convenient to use a product feature/benefit analysis, which also helps to differentiate features and benefits. Something of this process is shown in Table 9. Such an analysis can be produced for each product, or for a product range, and is perhaps particularly useful for new products. Again, this is an exercise that can be shown within an office, or section, to spread the task and help everyone to learn just what is a feature and what is a benefit.

Note that not all the needs will be objective ones. Most buyers, including industrial ones, also have subjective requirements bound up in their decisions. The graph in Figure 15 illustrates this concept: the line does not touch either axis as no product is bought on an entirely objective or subjective basis. Sometimes, even with technical products, the final decision can be heavily influenced by subjective factors, perhaps seemingly of minor significance, once all the objective needs have been met.

By matching benefits to individual customer needs, you are more likely to make a sale, for a product's benefits must match a buyer's needs. The features are only what give a product the right benefits.

By going through this process for particular products, and for segments of the range, and matching the factors identified to customer needs, a complete 'databank' of product information from the customers' viewpoint can be organised.

Using the benefit approach

With competitive products becoming increasingly similar, more buyers quickly conclude that their main needs can be met by more than one product. Other needs then become more important. If, for instance, a buyer needs a crane, he is likely to find a number of them which will lift the weight required, and which will also cost practically the same.

Customer needs	Benefits that will satisfy customer needs	Product features from which the benefits are derived
Rational		
(a) Performance – must be able to work fast with a variety of implements	Plenty of power, particularly at low speeds	A 65-BHP diesel engine with high torque at low rpm; wide range of matched implements available
(b) Versatility – must cope with a variety of soil and cultivating conditions	Can travel at a wide variety of speeds	A 10-speed synchromesh gearbox – four-wheel drive available for very difficult conditions
(c) Simplicity – must be easy to operate	Simple and speedy implement changeover; easy to drive	Quick-attach linkage with snap-on hydraulic couplings; ergonomically placed levers and pedals
(d) Low cost – must be economical to run	Low fuel consumption	Efficient engine design with improved braking and fuel injector system; good power/weight ratio
(e) Reliability – must be able to operate continuously and be serviced quickly	Well-proven design with all basic snags removed; local dealer with 24-hour parts service	More than 10,000 units already in operation; wide dealer network with factory-trained mechanics backed by computerised parts operation
Emotional		
(a) Security – (fear of making wrong decision)	Most popular tractor on the market – 10,000 farmers can't be wrong	Largest company in the industry with good reputation for reliability and value for money
(b) Prestige – (desire to gain status in the eyes of others)	Chosen by those engaged in best agricultual practice	Favoured by agricultural colleges and large farmers

Notes

1 The product analysis should be completed from left to right. Only when the needs have been identified can the appropriate benefits and the relevant features be selected.

2 If the salesman works from right to left not only will he lose his buyer's interest as he talks about items which may not be of interest, but also he will have no basis for selecting which benefits to stress.

3 This example is not intended as a complete analysis. That can only be done with a specific buyer in mind as each person has an individual need pattern. Performance will be most important to one farmer, low cost to another.

4 It will be noted that some of the product features are so technical as to be almost meaningless to the layman. This is one of the greatest dangers for the industrial salesman. Unless he translates his trade jargon he will fail to achieve understanding and thus cannot be persuasive.

Table 9. *Product feature/benefit analysis for an agricultural tractor*
(This chart is taken from *Managing a Sales Force* by Mike Wilson, of Marketing Improvements Group)

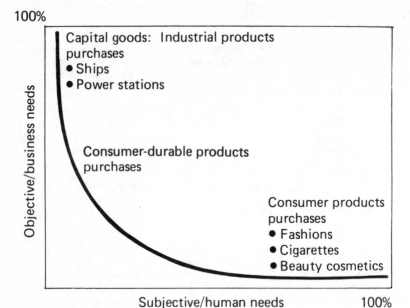

Figure 15. *Subjective/objective reasons for buying*

The deciding factors will then become availability, service and repair facilities, and so on. As a seller you can look at the 'features' contained by the company as a whole and be ready to convert them to benefits to customers, in the same way as you can practise finding benefits for the full product range. The aspects are all sources of benefits to customers. Four sources of benefits, and their aspects, are:

Products:	design	storage
	price	workmanship
	delivery	credit
	appearance	stocks
	packaging	
Services	speed	training
	availability	advertising
	credit	merchandising
	after-sales service	pre-sales advise
Companies:	time established	labour relations
	reputation	size
	location	policies

Staff:	philosophy	financial standing
	knowledge	availability
	skill	training
	character	specialists

Each item listed above could be a source of benefit to potential customers, which would help to make them an actual customer. By 'thinking benefits' and by seeing things from the customer's point of view, everyone can make a real contribution to sales and company profitability.

Jargon

A final hazard, which can destroy the customer orientation of your sales contacts, is jargon. This comes in two main forms, both of which can confuse customers:

Technical or industrial jargon. You should always let the customer be first to use it. Technological complexities have already led to thousands of new words and phrases in business and industry, and introducing still more new terms seldom helps. But worst of all is the possibility that the customer will not know what you are talking about, or will form the wrong impression, yet still hesitate to admit it.

Company jargon. It is even more important to avoid company jargon, for here the customer will be on very unfamiliar ground. There is a world of differences between 'We'll do a sales/stock return compo and the computer chappie will feed into the fourth floor, so we can let you know very shortly' and 'To answer your query, we'll have to do a comparison of the sales and stock return movements. The quickest way will be to ask for a computer print-out which Head Office will forward to us. I will contact you with the answer in a week or ten days time.'

Company jargon can affect everything you deal with, and even simple phrases can cause trouble. For example, delivery is one area for potential misunderstanding. Promising 'immediate delivery' might, in your terms, mean getting the product to the customer within a week, for normal delivery might take three weeks. But what if the customer is in the pharmaceutical industry, where 'immediate delivery' is jargon for 'within eight hours'? He is almost bound to get the wrong impression.

The right questions

Knowing how and why customers buy is a prerequisite to successful selling, and because all customers are individuals and want to be treated as such, selling must be based on finding out exactly what each customer wants, and why. In other words, questioning (and listening to and using the answers) is as important to selling as simply presenting our case.

It is important, therefore, to start asking questions early in the approach, and asking the right questions is crucial. Two characteristics are important in getting it right. They should be:

- *Open questions*: Those that cannot be answered by 'yes' or 'no', but get the customer talking. These work best and produce the most useful information.
- *Probing questions*: those that go beyond enquiring about the background situation, to explore problems and implications, and to identify real needs.

Let's return to the travel agent, Walter, for an example of the questioning technique he might use in conversation with a prospect.

Example 31. Questioning techniques

Agent: 'What areas are currently your priority Mr Export Manager?
Prospect: 'The Middle East is top priority for investigation but, short term, Germany has been more important.'
Agent: 'What makes that so?'
Prospect: 'Well we're exhibiting at a trade fair in Germany. This will tie up a number of staff and eat up a lot of the budget. Our exploratory visit to the Middle East may have to wait.'
Agent: 'Won't that cause problems, seeing as you had intended to go earlier?'
Prospect: 'I suppose it will. With the lead times involved it may rule out the chances of tying up any deals for this financial year.'
Agent: 'Had you thought of moving one of your people straight on from Germany to the Middle East, Mr Export Manager?'
Prospect: 'Er, no.'
Agent: 'I think I could show some real savings over making two separate trips. If you did it this way, the lead time wouldn't slip. Would that be of interest?'
Prospect: 'Could be. If I give you some dates can we map something out to show exactly how it could be done?'
Agent: 'Certainly . . . '

This kind of questioning not only produces information but can be used creatively to spot opportunities. It accurately pin-points the prospect's real needs and allows an accurate response to them. Most prospects not only like talking about their own situation but react favourably to this approach. They may well see the genuine identification of their problems and the offer of solutions to them as distinctly different to any competitive approach .they have received, which simply catalogues the product or services offered.

In this case, it also allows much better demonstration of two benefits that purchasers look for from travel agents: objectivity and expertise. The more these are apparent, the more the agency is differentiated from the competition.

If the right deal is offered to the prospect in the right way, he ceases to be a prospect and becomes a customer. So far so good. What next?

Customer service

As has already been mentioned, it is increasingly difficult for customers to differentiate between competing products in the market. In many industries, such products are essentially similar in terms of design, performance and specification, at least within a given price bracket. This is as true of industrial products as consumer goods. Often, customers' final·choices will, therefore, be influenced by more subjective areas. Customer services can play a major role in this, sometimes becoming the most important factor.

For example, in the authors' own company, the source of ring binders used for the many courses and seminars we conduct was, for a while, influenced almost exclusively, in a commodity-type product area with many suppliers offering similar products, by the efficiency and customer orientation of one girl in the suppliers' sales office. When she left them, the business was subsequently moved elsewhere. The antithesis of this is the 'abominable noman' who too often seems to inhibit the sales office. He can destroy months of work by management and sales staff, miss opportunities and lose orders or indeed customers, in a moment, maybe in one brief telephone call.

So how can you get it right and maximise the impact inside sales support staff have on sales results? Primarily by careful consideration of both staffing and organisation. It is not easy. The mix of characteristics and considerations that can help make success more likely is not easy to define:

- It is not enough for the manager only to be a good administrator, although without the sorting out of priorities, without smooth handling of enquiries, files, paperwork, correspondence and records, sales support will never be effective.

- It is not enough for him only to be a good sales person, although it is essential to have an understanding of familiarity with sales techniques, be able to recognise sales opportunities, and ensure both he and members of his team meet them.
- It is not enough for him only to be an effective manager of people, although it is vital to be able to lead and motivate a close-knit and enthusiastic team, tackling a diverse range of activity in hectic conditions.

The manager also has to understand and pass on an understanding of the role of sales support, so that all concerned see it as a vital tactical weapon in the overall marking operation. This means that he must have an appreciation of what marketing is and the various ways in which, directly or indirectly, the sales office can contribute to company profitability.

This implies a knowledge of, and involvement in, the marketing process. For example, if sales support personnel are not told (or do not ask about) the relative profitability of different products, they may be busy pushing product 'A' when product 'B', similar in price or even more expensive, makes more money.

A pre-requisite for contributing effectively is for any manager to be able to identify priorities. With such a variety of activities, with incoming calls and enquiries being so unpredictable, the manager either adheres to rigid sets of rules that allow things to be coped with and runs an adequate office, or he has the skill and initiative to recognise different priorities and to get the best out of them, so building up a really effective operation.

Identifying priorities is of little use, however, unless the manager is able to organise to deal with them. This calls for abilities in managing and controlling time, systems and people.

To be effective he must be a consistent sales-oriented manager of people, able to accept ideas from others, able to cope with the problems of the urgent and balance this with the opportunities of the important.

The sales support team must be organised to produce an ongoing positive cycle of repeat business from its contacts. Even negative contacts such as complaints can be dealt with as part of a positive cycle involving a range of possible contacts with the customer, either directly or through other sections of the company. Although possibly low among company priorities, sales support in fact occupies a central position, which is vital in terms of contacts and influence.

For this to occur may require close and constructive co-operation with other sections of the company) for example, pro-duction, sales force. Poor liason can cause problems. In one company, for instance, sales office staff spent time handling com-plaints about delivery on 75 per cent of orders that went through, not because delivery was bad, but because the sales force was quoting six weeks delivery when everyone in the company knew it was eight weeks. Such unnecessarily wasted time could be used more constructively to increase sales.

There are of course exceptions: prevailing standards of sales office service and selling are not high. It should not be difficult, therefore, to make customer contact not only stand out in a way that really impresses customers but which genuinely increases sales results. For many small firms, this is a real opportunity area.

There are no excuses for not selling. Time pressure, work pressure, staffing, equipment and resources may all make it more difficult, but what in fact ensures real selling does take place is, first, attitude and, second, knowledge and skills of how to do it ef-fectively. Only management can get this over and maintain stan-dards. It is, in fact, much easier to run a 'tight ship' to set standards and stick to them than to let things go by default. People are motivated by belonging to the 'best team' and come to care about standards and performance very much.

Selling must not be confused with simple customer service, however efficient and courteous. This is not to deny the vital im-portance of service and courteousness. This forms one of the bases for success, but so does product knowledge – not just knowing about the product, but being able to talk about it in such a way that makes sense to the customer. This does not just happen. Management must ensure that it does, and similarly with sales technique. The sales office team (all of them who have customer contact) must have a basic knowledge of the sales process augmented by knowledge of and ability to apply particular skills, on the telephone or in letter writing for instance, and backed as necessary by sheer persistence and inventiveness. Again, this does not just happen. Management is responsible for recruiting the right people, their initial training and on-going development, and for motivating them on a continuous basis. As with so many topics reviewed here, customer service and the internal sales effort have more to them than meets the eye. Yet think about organisations you do business with, as a company or as an individual. There is always one about which you say 'never again!' and others where good service draws you back time after time, probably without your thinking that you have been sold to in a 'pushy' manner. To demonstrate this kind of selling in practice, perhaps we can conclude by mentioning that the whole area of sales support is covered in Patrick Forsyth's book *Running an Effective Sales Office*.

Holding and developing customers

There is an old saying that 'selling starts when the customer says yes' meaning that if you want long-term, repeat business, you must work at it. Again, the principles can be illustrated by reference to the travel agent Walter.

Example 32. Holding and developing customers

Walter knows that in winning more business travel the overall objective is not one order, but on-going profitable business from this area. Whether customers are retained, buy again and buy more is dependent primarily on two factors:

- *Service*: It almost goes without saying, but promises of service must be fulfilled to the letter; if they are not, the customer will notice. A number of different people may be involved in servicing the account. They all have to appreciate the importance and get their bit right.

    If the customer was promised information by 3.30pm, a visa by the end of the week, two suggested itineraries in writing and a re-servation in a certain hotel at a particular price, then he should get just that. Even minor variations, such as information by 4pm and a slight price difference on room rate, do matter. Promise what can be done. And do it 100 per cent.

- *Follow-up*: Even if the service received is first class, the customer must continue to be sold to after the order as follows:
    - Check with him after his trip.
    - Check who else is involved in the next purchase. His secretary? Other managers?
    - Ask more questions. When is his next trip? When should he be contacted again?
    - Make suggestions. Can he book earlier? Would he like to take his wife on his next trip?
    - Anticipate. Does he know fares are going up? Can he make the trip earlier and save money?
    - Explore what else he might buy.
    - Investigate who else in the company travels. Other staff, depart-ments, subsidiaries?
    - See whether you can distribute holiday information among his staff.
    - Write to him, do not let him forget you. Make sure he thinks of you first.

A positive follow-up programme of this sort can maximise the chances of repeat business and ensure that opportunities to sell additional products or services are not missed.

The sales team

All the topics reviewed have been done so without specific reference to the number of sales staff involved. Indeed, initially the owner of a small business may do it all. But as the business grows, additional sales resources may be necessary. Some will be inside staff, already mentioned under customer service, others may be field sales force. While sales management is very much part of marketing, it is a well-documented one; suffice it to say here that the sales manager has responsibilities for planning and organising the sales resources, for recruiting, training and motivating the team, and controlling their efforts. This is a complex body of skills, techniques and tasks, and is worth fuller study at a stage where your business makes it appropriate. '*Managing a Sales Force*' by Mike Wilson is the text the authors would suggest, not least because of its practical approach.

Checklist

- Do you recognise selling as an active element of your communication mix?
- Have you identified everyone in the company who has a sales role to play? Are you sure they perform this role satisfactorily?
- Do you have a rolling plan to identify prospects? Do you systematically use all the sources of information that will make such a plan effective? Do you deploy the right person to follow up leads/prospects?
- Does everyone in the company with customer contact responsibilities know the product/service background? Can they describe the product from the customers' point of view (benefits/features)? Does on-going briefing on product knowledge occur, when, how and as often as necessary?
- Do all concerned think first and foremost in terms of customer needs? Is there too much jargon used in communicating with customers?
- Is the sales and back-up support a managed activity so that it delivers the right standard of performance all the time? Do you lose any customers by default or through neglect?

Part 4
Synthesis and Conclusion

10
Controlling the Marketing Operation

Control is the process by which you ensure that you accomplish what you have set out to achieve. What, then, are the marketing operations trying to achieve?

In the past, marketing operations and activities were simply judged by whether they increased sales or not. Given the wider definition of marketing adopted in this book, this oversimplifies what the marketing approach is trying to achieve. Marketing activities have as their objective the long-term profitable survival of the firm, and it is by this criterion that the success or otherwise of your marketing operation should be judged.

Control means much more than judgement of whether you have been successful at the end of the year. Managers have to manage. They have to ensure that the right activities are in motion today, which will bring about the results wanted at the end of the period. To control, therefore, managers need to:

- set standards of performance in the key areas;
- collect information about the performance being achieved;
- compare what performance is being achieved with what must be achieved;
- take action to bring performance back to standard.

Let us examine each activity in turn.

Setting standards of performance in the key areas

Standards of performance are the controls by which you are going to run the marketing operations. They resemble, in many ways, the control systems a driver uses to monitor the engine performance of his car. In a car, a well-designed instrument panel will consist of a series of controls, which:

- Monitor all causes of failure.

There are several hundred causes of engine failure. All these malfunctions will, however, manifest themselves in the systems measured, such as level of petrol in the tank, engine temperature, electrics, oil pressure.

- Help diagnosis.

Since all the causes of failure are thus grouped under electrical, fuel, etc, the major controls will help to narrow down the fault to a specific set of causes, thus saving time in pin-pointing the trouble.

- Do not distract when all is well.

As the controls continuously monitor the essential functions, they only attract attention when a process has moved from the standard set; for example, a drop in oil pressure will show up only when it has reached a critical level. In business terms this is known as managing by exception.

- Give advance warning of problems developing, to give time to take corrective action.

The use of management ratio analysis
A most useful approach to developing this type of instrument panel for managing the marketing operation has been developed and implemented by MT Wilson,* with considerable success. The technique starts with a consideration of the overall profitability you would like to achieve. It then moves to the development of a series of measures that will not only signal whether operations will result in a decrease (or increase) in profitability, but which operations are causing the problem, so there is time to take corrective action.

Setting overall profitability targets
To implement this control system, you need first to express the overall company profitability you are aiming for in terms that can be used for control. Thus, expressing profitability as a certain number of thousands of pounds is not exact enough. Unless you relate this to the amount of capital needed to generate it, you will have no idea whether it is difficult or easy to achieve.

---

* See MT Wilson *Managing a Sales Force*, Gower Press.

Consensus now seems to be reached that for management control purposes, the most useful expression of profitability is the Return on Capital Employed (or ROCE), expressed as:

$$\text{ROCE} = R/CE = \text{Return}/\text{Capital employed}$$
$$= \frac{[\text{Profit before tax and interest charges}]}{[\text{Total assets} - \text{Current liabilities}]}$$

Normally as a percentage, so this fraction needs to be multiplied by 100. The profit before tax figure will appear on your financial income statement. The total assets and current liabilities on your balance sheet.

This ratio can be developed into two other ratios by a common algebraic device; namely, multiplying by a figure divided by itself and transposed. In this case, the figure is the annual sales (S), as follows:

$$R/CE = R/CE \times S/S$$

which transposed gives:

$$R/CE = R/S \times S/CE$$

For example, if R = £10, CE = £100 and S = £200, then:

$$R/CE = 10/100 = 1/10 = 10\%$$
$$= 10/100 \times 200/200$$

Transposing:

$$R/CE = 10/200 \times 200/100 = 1/10 = 10\%$$
$$= 10/200 \times 200/100$$
$$= 5\% \times 2 = 10\%$$

two new ratios have now been derived which are both useful measures. The ratio:

$$R/S$$

gives the return on sales (or ROS). Again, ROS is normally expressed as a percentage. A moments' thought will show you that this is your gross profit margin. If this deteriorates, so will your ROCE. If the ROS went down to say, 9, this would have an immediate effect upon ROCE as follows:

$$\text{ROCE} = R/S \times S/CE$$
$$= 9/200 \times 200/100 = 9\%$$

The ratio:

$$S/CE$$

describes the capital turnover rate (CTR).

This is the rate at which the firm's capital is turned over in a year. CTR is normally expressed preceded by a multiplication sign. For example, '×3' indicates that the capital is turned over three times in a year.

The importance of this ratio is crucial in the retail trade, for example, where the largest part of the capital is in the form of stock. If, in the example given earlier, the owner of the store increased his stock and thus his capital to 150, but sales did not increase, his results would look like this:

$$\text{ROCE} = R/S \times S/CE = {}^{10}/_{200} \times {}^{200}/_{150} = 6\%$$

Any change in the profitability of the firm will show up in one or both of these ratios, making diagnosis much easier than working from ROCE alone.

The ratios of ROS and CTR can now be developed further into a family of indicators, as shown below, to enable you to pin-point not simply why, say, ROS has declined, but how it has declined.

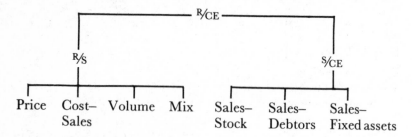

The factors affecting ROS

There are only four factors that can adversely effect the gross profit margin, or ROS. They are:

- The prices charged are too low.
- The costs have risen faster than your prices.
- The volume of sales has been too low.
- The product mix has deteriorated.

Let us consider each in turn.

Price. Chapter 6 showed how cost plus mark-up pricing can result in prices that are too low. Having once set the price, it can be eroded for several different reasons, as follows:

- You are nervous of asking the optimum price, whereas research indicates that customers are often far less concerned about the asking price than is the seller. Good salesmanship can often help here.
- You do not use the opportunities for differential pricing strategies and charge all customers the same no matter how much extra work or effort may be involved.
- You are reluctant to pass on cost increases in higher prices, for fear of losing customers who you have expended so much effort in attracting. As a result, you may well have filled your books with customers who only use you because your price is low.
- Where you give discounts for larger sales, they may not be adequately compensated for by the savings you are making by supplying in bulk.

Costs. The ratios indicate that there are several reasons why costs may have eaten into your profits and have not been compensated for by higher sales. Every element of your offering, however, needs to be carefully examined to see if extra costs are contributing to extra sales, as discussed in Chapter 5. If it does not contribute extra sales, you should consider cutting out that extra feature. Some examples of cost increases follow:

- Have you built features into your product which are not even perceived by the customer?
- Are you offering services that have had no effect upon sales? Did you check whether your customers will pay more for a new service before you introduced it?
- Are you trying to offer a delivery service that is far more costly than your customers need?
- Are you using the right selling methods? Could selling be done more cheaply by other means, such as telephone selling or promotion?

Volume too low. If your fixed costs are high, you have to sell more before you have covered your costs. Another business running on lower fixed costs by, for example, renting or leasing, rather than buying premises or equipment, is making profits before you are.

Any increase in fixed costs, unless it results in higher sales or lower overall costs, is bound to deflate the ROS. You need to reflect very carefully, therefore, before you inflict extra burdens on your business.

Product mix deteriorated. As you have seen in Chapter 5, the various lines that make up the product mix may yield very different profit margins. Even if your total sales figures have not changed, if you sell more of the low margin items and less of the high margin, your ROS will deteriorate. Some examples of where you can improve your performance are:

- Do you measure your success by sales volume or do you measure it by contribution?
- In your promotion do you concentrate on those lines that yield the best margin or those that are easiest to sell?
- If you are employing sales staff, do you indicate the 'priority lines' – those that have the best margins? Do you reward them accordingly?

The factors affecting CTR
There are three factors that are of major concern to marketing operations; namelv:

- stocks
- debtors
- fixed assets.

Let us deal with these in turn.

Stocks. Although the control of stocks is not directly a marketing task, marketing decisions can directly affect the level of stocks, particularly finished stocks, as follows:

- Where new lines are introduced and old lines are not phased out, stocks may rise faster than sales
- When a product is being phased out, there is always a temptation to oblige a customer by keeping stocks especially for him, even though the turnround of these stocks may be particularly low. This will affect your profit unless these extra financing costs are met by higher prices to that customer, or else suggesting he keeps his own stock of such products.
- If you want to provide a better-than-ordinary service as a manufacturer or retailer, your stock level will be higher than average. Unless this is reflected in higher volumes of sales or higher prices, your CTR will deteriorate and will not be offset by a better return on the ROS.

Debtors. Debtors are those customers who have not yet paid their bills. If you give customers longer to pay, your total debtor figure will rise accordingly. You may be often tempted to use credit as a means of getting business. If you do, however, this will worsen your CTR and profitability will have to be made up elsewhere. Points to ponder include:

- Do you give longer credit to your bigger customers? Does the extra business justify the cost?
- Are you giving more credit to achieve the same amount of sales?
- Are you doing more business with poor payers?
- Do you make those who take longer to pay pay extra?

Fixed assets. If new fixed assets have been acquired, but are not yet producing a return, CTR will similarly be affected. Similarly, if existing fixed assets are underutilised, this ratio will deteriorate. A managerial decision is therefore required to assess whether the decreased profitability will be tolerated or steps should be taken to compensate for this problem.

Collecting information about the performance being achieved

Once you have identified the key factors you need to monitor the business, you can set up your internal information system, which enables you to act promptly to take corrective action.

A skilled restaurateur, for example, instead of worrying whether he will make a profit or not by the end of the year, sets up controls to measure how he is doing on a day-to-day basis. Working with his accountant, he calculates the average size of customer orders, and then the number of seats he has to fill to cover his costs. One glance at the number of customers in the dining room will tell him whether or not he is making a profit on that day. By extension, he has another measure that tells him whether he is reaching his profit target. He is thus able to take prompt corrective action to bring his sales back to target.

A machine tool salesman has a different problem. His annual sales, although substantial, consisted of a small number of large orders. To obtain his business, he normally has to make a large number of prospecting calls to determine who could use the equipment and their requirements. A certain proportion of these surveys lead to quotations and some, but not all of these quotations, lead to orders. An analysis of his results over the last year reveals the following:

No of visits	Prospecting surveys	No of quotations	No of orders
240	60	12	3

To achieve one order, on balance, by dividing all the above figures by 3, he arrives at the following requirements:

Prospecting visits	Surveys	Quotations	Orders
80	20	4	1

He has set next year's business at four orders; therefore, he requires:

Annual Standards

Prospecting visits	Surveys	Quotations	Orders
320	80	16	4

To control his business, he needs to translate these figures into weekly standards. He does this by dividing the above by 50 and rounding up to the nearest whole number, giving:

Weekly Standards

Prospecting visits	Surveys	Quotations
7	2	1

He can now take steps to ensure that whichever part of his performance has fallen behind, be it prospecting, surveys or quotations, he can take action to bring it back on to target before it is too late.

Comparing the performance being achieved with what must be achieved

Often, a simple comparison between the standards set and the results can mislead you. A large order coming in late or another coming in early can distort one month's sales figures and mislead you. Some form of 'smoothing' is thus necessary to ensure that you do not over-react to an abnormal situation.

One approach is to set parameters within which the results can be allowed to vary without requiring action. In the machine tool salesman example, prospecting visits could vary with ± 2 within a given week without results really being affected, and so variations of this magnitude are ignored. The problem with this approach is that the shortfall can accumulate and become serious without the system picking it up.

There are several techniques for overcoming this problem, some using averaging and some cumulative techniques. The most useful, the Z chart, combines both approaches and will provide a clear picture of what is happening to any of the variables that affect your business, although its most common use is to control sales.

The Z chart

This system uses three measures:

- the monthly sales figures;
- the cumulative monthly figures;
- the moving annual total (MAT).

Figure 16 (top) illustrates how it is developed.

At the start of the year, two figures are inserted:

- the annual target for the current year (in this case £50,000);
- the annual total for the previous year (in this case £40,000).

As the monthly results come in, they are first plotted into the chart in the normal way to show the 'monthly results' for each month. In this instance, they are shown for January, February, March and April at the bottom of the chart.

The 'cumulative' monthly results line can be developed at the same time by plotting:

- at January, the January results:
- at February, the sum of the January plus February results;
- at March, the sum of the January plus March results, etc.

Finally, the moving annual averages can be developed by adding the results for the previous 11 months to each months' figures and plotting them at the top of the graph, as follows:

- at January, the January results and previous year's results from February to December;

- at February, the February results and the previous year's results for March to January;
- at March, the March results plus the previous year's results from April to February, etc.

At the end of the year, the 'moving annual average' line meets the cumulative monthly line in December to complete the Z shape of the three graphs. Figure 16 (bottom) shows, however, that both the MAT and monthly cumulative lines meet at a point below the annual sales target for this year and extra effort is required if a shortfall is not to occur. All in all, a great deal of information from one chart.

Take action to bring performance back to standard

When running your own business, you are always short of time. It is essential that you practise management by exception as far as possible; that is, in the planning process you need to develop a clear set of performance standards and an information system that enables you to measure deviation from these standards with the minimum of fuss. You can then concentrate on correcting deviations from standard.

When deviations do occur, however, action is required promptly, as follows:

- First, identify if it is the plan or the execution of the plan which is at fault.
- If it is the execution, it is either the system or the people operating the system which is at fault.
- If you are to train and develop staff, you need to give them specific goals to reach within a specific time period and give them every opportunity to achieve that level of performance.
- If after that they are unable to reach the required standards, they will need to be replaced.

Checklist

- Do you have a profitability target?
- Can your accountant help you to calculate it in terms of ROCE?
- Can you calculate the target ROS and CTR for your firm?
- Examine the causes of a deteriorating ROS. What steps will you take to ensure this does not happen to your firm?
- Examine the factors affecting CTR. How will you monitor these factors?

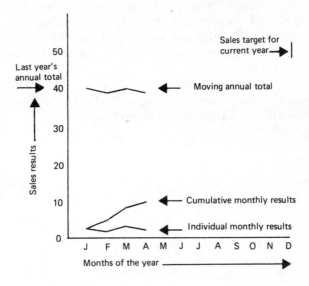

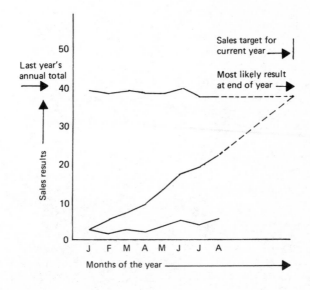

Figure 16. *The development of a Z chart*

- Do you have any of rules of thumb, such as the restaurateur or machine tool salesman have developed, to help your run your business? Can your accountant help you develop some?
- Develop a Z chart for your business. Where does it point towards? A shortfall or an overshoot on target? What are you going to do about it?
- When targets were not achieved last time, how did you go about taking corrective action? Which system will you introduce to take action in future?

Appendices

Appendix 1
National Readership Survey: Social Status Groups

Social grade	Social status	Occupation of head of household	Percentage of total UK population
A	Upper middle	Top managerial, administrative professional	3.1
B	Middle	Intermediate managerial professional administrative	13.4
C1	Lower middle	Supervisory clerical, junior managerial	22.3
C2	Skilled working class	Skilled manual workers	31.2
D	Working class	Semi-skilled, unskilled manual workers	19.1
E	Lowest levels of subsistence	widows, state pensioners, casual labour	10.9

Appendix 2

Sources of Market Information

Source	Type of information	Possible uses
Firm's own sources Order book, invoice file, enquiries, complaints, sales visit reports	Average size of order, length of payment period, type of customer most attracted, quotation to order ratio (see Chapter 10), geographical distribution of customers (and, by extension, which areas are not successful)	Invaluable source of information for controlling the operation, to monitor changes over time, status with competitors, strengths, and weaknesses
Official sources (a) *Government Publications* *Annual Abstract of Statistics*, special Government investigations	Rate of production, stocks, prices and sales for major industries, regions, and the economy as whole; import statistics; general economic indicators, eg where 'housing starts' exceed 'housing completions' the economy is bouncing back	General information on whether the economy is picking up, or particular industries and regions are recovering or declining, or may be worth considering entering

Source	Type of information	Possible uses
(b) *Local government* Borough engineers' office, rating office, PR department, industrial development office, education department, reference libraries	Lists and statistics of: numbers of children in education and locality; future trends; adults with names and addresses; all applications for building permission; economic development studies commisioned by the local authority; forward plans for development of the area	Invaluable early warning of developments in area; good source of consumer mailing lists; consult also the local press for applications, advertisements for staff, news of economic developments
(c) *Companies House* Business sections of newspapers	Annual company financial statements; chairmen's reports on outlook for firm and past year's results	Where a small number of firms dominate an industry, a region or suppliers; the decisions these firms take will have a pronounced effect on other firms' futures
Private associations *(a)* *Trade associations*	Industrial indicators of average profitability financial soundness, etc; industrial forecasts	Most trade associations gather a wide range of information for their members, and thus can save them a lot of time consulting a wide range of other

Source	Type of information	Possible uses
		sources; index of all UK trade associations, available in most reference libraries, will help you spot the most appropriate association for your purpose
(b) *Banks and financial houses*	Economic analysis overseas intelligence; financial intelligence	Most banks provide a wide variety of general and specific economic analysis free; they will often provide specific confidential information on prospective distributors or customers
(c) *Dun & Bradstreet*	Undertake specific investigations into the financial viability of customers/suppliers/ competitors on behalf of banks or clients	Help to set limits to length and amount of credit for individual customers or distributors; advice on whether a specific distributor has the finance to grow as you would like
(d) *Technical press*	New technologies, specific research into industries	New product development technologies which might make your service or product obsolete or help you improve it

Source	Type of information	Possible uses
Market research publications (a) *ITV regional marketing handbooks*	Detailed demographic, economic, marketing information based on reports prepared to convince advertisers of the advantages of advertising to that region	A wide variety of uses since it compares national with regional figures and assembles that information from a variety of sources with references so that you can dig out more detailed information as necessary
(b) *Specific studies Mintel, Retail Business, Euromonitor*	Does in-depth studies the markets for individual products showing competitors' markets, shares, etc	Where these studies have been carried out, they are essential reading for market potential or industry studies and will provide a high proportion of the information necessary for decision making
Keynote Publications	Specific research into buying habits of social groups with forecasts	

Source	Type of information	Possible uses
(c) *Specific lists and indices*	Kompass lists all UK manufacturing and commercial firms, giving addresses, telephone numbers, size and type of manufacture or service	Invaluable guides for direct mail shots, planning sales campaigns, identifying market characteristics
	Kelly's Directory Based on a geographical basis, shows the location of each manufacturing commercial establishment	Planning sales routes and journeys
	British Rate and Data Lists all forms of advertising media, TV, newspapers, magazines, transport advertising, etc; shows the costs of each and the kind of people who watch or read them	All advertising and promotion planning

Appendix 3

The Use of Market Research in Setting Up a New Business

Brian wanted to combine a hobby with a career. As a wine buff of many years standing, he wished to set up a new kind of wine outlet which concentrated on fine wines only. His research followed three stages and finally he arrived at a statement of:

- his annual sales
- his total investment.

Let us examine each stage in turn.

Defining the concept of the business

Before Brian could clarify his own mind as to how this new kind of fine wine centre would work, he needed to establish via a series of exploratory discussions:

- what kind of person enjoyed fine wines (age, social group, etc);
- what they were looking for in pursuing this interest (low price, interest in different wines, information, etc);
- their degree of satisfaction with present sources of supply of fine wines and information about them.

After 20 or so discussions, certain facts became clear, as follows:

- An interest in fine wines, as opposed to wines in general, was concentrated on the AB groups in that area and was growing.
- Their basic interest in wine was not confined to obtaining wines they already knew, but in finding out about different vineyards and vintages and tasting these wines.

- There was no clear favourite way of finding out about fine wines. Most followed television programmes, read books on the subject and explored wine cellars in the city. In each case, they felt that these approaches were unsatisfactory. The wine cellars, particularly, were, they felt, filled with 'wine snobs' who were pretentious, unhelpful and unknowledgeable.
- There was a need for a wine cellar that was centrally located, at which seminars and tastings could be held, and wines discussed and served.

Overall 'macro' research

Since Brian would be committing his career to this trade, he wanted to know if he was joining a growing business opportunity or a stagnating or ephemeral phenomenon.

Consulting *government statistics* indicated that the demand for beer was strongly in decline, whereas for quality wine was rising rapidly. Consulting the *Journal of Retail Business*, he found a recent survey of the drinks market, which gave extremely interesting figures, as follows:

- which segments of the market were growing fastest;
- which kind of outlet sold most (off licence, on licence, supermarket, etc);
- which kind of packaging (bottled, bulk, wine box) was growing fastest;
- where wine was consumed (at home, in clubs, pubs, etc);
- who decided which brand was chosen (wife, husband, etc).

From these figures, it was clear that supermarkets dominated the low price bulk wine trade and it would be wise to distance his business from what they were trying to do. Fine wines required personal advice which was not being provided by them and they were not really geared up to enter the market.

While dealing with government statistics, he thought it would be useful to identify what the balance of his stock should be: that is, the proportion of white, red and rosé, and how much French, Italian, Spanish and German he should stock. The relevant import figures by country and type were, therefore, extremely useful.

The local market

Brian had several problems to solve in the area he wished to centre his business, as follows:

- How many of the target group were in the area?
- How did these prospective customers spend their money?
- What were their leisure habits (visits to restaurants, entertaining at home, etc)?

The local ITV regional marketing handbook provided the answers to all these questions. The first question was a little more complex than he first thought. Although he had the figures for the target group in the area, he needed to know how many would shop in the country town in which he intended to locate his business. The question had two aspects therefore:

- How large was the target population in the town itself?
- How large was the target population who *visited* the town to do their shopping?

Brian found that a *survey* had been commissioned by the borough to identify from which secondary area the town drew its shoppers, what type of shopping they came to town to do and whether there were enough shopping facilities to cope with the demand.

Quantifying the results

From the information obtained, Brian calculated the following:

Population who live within ½ hour drive of town	500,000
of which 30% travel to town to shop	166,667
of which 16% are AB social category	26,667
Population of town	120,000
of which 16% are AB social category*	19,667
Target AB population	45,867

How many will respond to direct mail?	
Journals indicate about 2½%	1,147
How much will they buy per year?	
Secondary research indicates 1 bottle per week	
@ £10 each; therefore, annual turnover	£596,440
Gross profit @ 20%	£119, 288

---

* This figure is below the national average (see Appendix 1).

Investment in stock
  Discussions with trade indicates stock will
  turn over about eight times per year; therefore,
  dividing annual sales figure by 8, stock value   £74,555

Further expenses

Cost of rented premises
  Figure available from estate agents   £5,000
Cost of publicity
  Calculated from postage and typing estimates   £2,000
Cost of staff
  from job centre   £15,000
Other expenses   £5,000
Total expenses   £27,000

At this point, Brian has the information necessary to justify to a
bank manager whether his scheme is feasible or not. From the
painstaking way he has gone about developing these figures, it is
clear that Brian is not guessing, but is forming his ideas on good
information and is likely to succeed.

Further Reading from Kogan Page

Be Your Own PR Man: Practical Public Relations for the Small Business, Michael Bland, 2nd edn 1987

Customer Service: How to Achieve Total Customer Satisfaction, Malcolm Peel, 1987

Do Your Own Market Research, Paul N Hague and Peter Jackson, 1987

Getting Sales: A Practical Guide to Getting More Sales for Your Business, R D Smith and G Dick, 1984

Effective Advertising for the Small Business, H C Carter, 1986

A Handbook of Advertising Techniques, Tony Harrison, 1987

How to Advertise, Kenneth Roman and Jane Maas, 1979

How to Promote Your Own Business: A Guide to Low Budget Publicity, Jim Dudley, 1987

The Industrial Market Research Handbook, Paul N Hague, 2nd edn 1987

Practical Sponsorship, Stuart Turner, 1987

Promoting Yourself on Television and Radio, Michael Bland and Simone Mondesir, 1987

Sales Training Basics: A Primer for Those New to Selling, Elwood N Chapman, 1988

Successful Marketing for the Small Business, Dave Patten, 2nd edn 1989

Ten Keys to Dynamic Customer Relations, Gregory H Sorensen, 1988

Index